I0203755

Photo by Bob and Bill Gadd

Six "whirleys" sit atop the framework that is slowly being devoured by the millions of tons of concrete that will complete Libby Dam

1975 – 2025
LIBBY DAM **50**th
COMMEMORATION

US Army Corps of Engineers®
Seattle District

Bold Legacy

ISBN 978-1-886591-38-7
Library of Congress Control Number: 2025943454

Printed in the United States of America

Operation BOLD was published to commemorate the 50th Anniversary of the Libby Dam by Blue Creek Press for the Libby Dam Cooperative Association, with financial assistance from the LOR Foundation.

LOR FOUNDATION

BLUE CREEK PRESS

Blue Creek Press
P.O. Box 110
Heron, MT 59844
books@bluecreekpress.com

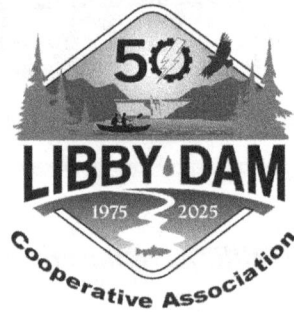

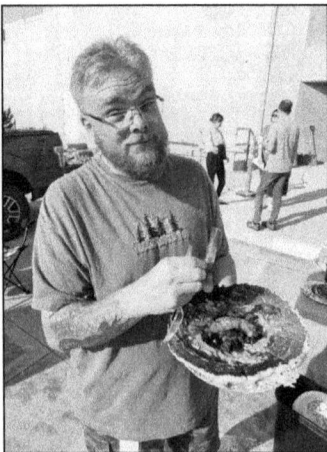

50
LIBBY DAM
1975   2025
Cooperative Association

About the Author: Rich Aarstad came to Kootenai Valley with his family in August 1966, just prior to Operation B.O.L.D. He graduated from Libby High in 1982, and spent several years behind the pickup window at Henry's Café. He met and married Kim Cummings in 1994 while attending the Lincoln County Campus of Flathead Valley Community College. He became aquainted with Libby Dam while working there as a seasonal employee. Rich and Kim now live near Winston, MT, where she enjoys retirement as he continues his work as State Archivist. Their son, Rick, lives in Spokane, WA, with their two precocious granddaughters, Chesnie Diane and Kashlyn Christine. He is a master of huckleberry pancakes and bacon.

Operation BOLD

Libby Dam at Fifty

By Rich [Ray] Aarstad

2000, 2025

Bold Legacy

Above: Construction is just beginning in 1969.

Below: Libby Dam today

This book contains over 130 photos and graphics,
the majority of which were scanned from the US Army Corps of Engineers
photo archives at Libby Dam. Others are attributed as appropriate.

Cover photo by Harold Carbine

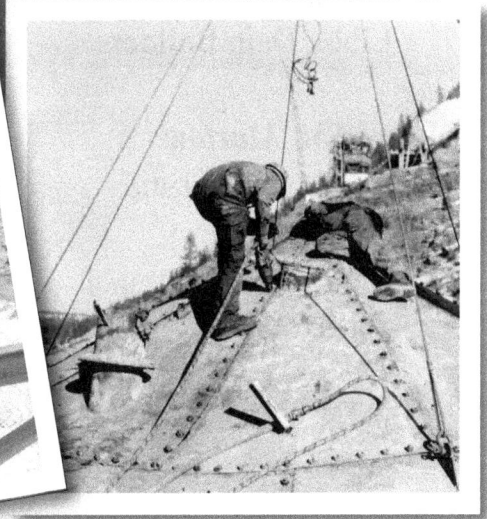

In Memory

As the residents of Lincoln County prepare for the 50th anniversary of the dedication of Libby Dam, this publication is dedicated to the memory of those individuals who died while working on the project, 1966-1975.

John Clyde Howe
July 31, 1967
Libby Dam Builders

Norris T. Halvorson
June 16, 1970
Stewart-Erickson
Highway 37

Fred H. Ingraham
February 29, 1968
Libby Dam Builders

Kenneth A. Hermanson
October 2, 1972
R.W. Reed Painters

Bill M. Marlow
November 6, 1968
Walsh-Grove
Elk Mountain Tunnel

Bill Peterson
March 12, 1973
Safety Inspector
Libby Dam

Cum gratia et amore

Merle S. Wallis
July 29, 1969
Libby Dam Builders

Frank Skranak
November 11, 1973
Stewart-Erickson

Charles C. Willems
August 18, 1969
Walsh-Grove
Elk Mountain Tunnel

Donald C. Lambert
July 20, 1973
Stewart-Erickson
Highway 37

Ray E. Willis
July 1, 1970
Columbia Basin Steel Co.
Libby Dam

Tom Surman
October 3, 1973
Stewart-Erickson
Highway 37

Table of Contents

Acknowledgments

This publication would not have happened without several people assisting from start to finish. Vicky Silcox, who asked if I would and waited patiently until I realized I could. Mick Shea wanted something about the history of the dam but not an historical monograph. Dick Wernham mentored a young historian and gave him room to succeed. Alana Mesenbrink, who became a close family friend, made sure the original manuscript stayed present and never let the original goal of getting it publish be forgotten.

Susan James saw an opportunity as the 50th anniversary approached of the dedication of Libby Dam to have the manuscript retooled and published. She and Jeff Gruber spent hours at the Libby Dam Vistors' Center scanning USACE photographs that were selected for the book and their efforts elevated the content to an amazing level. Sandy Compton and Blue Creek Press took an idea, photographs, and words on pages and created a work of art and in the process fulfilled a long held dream. All three did DAM good work. Thanks to Tabitha Viergutz and the LOR Foundation for the financial grants to publish this work of heart and history,.

Twenty-five years changes one's writing style, and the original manuscript needed a lot of help. My friend Scott Meredith, one of the most knowledgeable individuals I know, agreed to look it over and his comments proved invaluable. Batting cleanup, Terence Kratz, colleague and friend, put the polish to the final manuscript making it shine. Their efforts made this writing work.

Speaking of work, this book belongs to the individuals who made time for my questions and made introductions to others that make this narrative sing: Phil Cole, John Coyle, Miles Briggs, Gene Scalf, Don Smith, John Davidson, Bill Glenn, and Jim Morey. I hope I did you proud.

Any history of this region relies on the publications of Donald Spritzer, author of *Waters of Wealth: The Story of the Kootenai River and Libby Dam* and Jack Nisbet's *Sources of the River: Tracking David Thompson Across Western North America*. They remain the cornerstones of any history of the Kootenai River Valley, and without them, I would have been lost writing my own narrow history of the Libby Dam Project.

I'm sure there are others, but 25 years have dimmed the memory so my apologies to those I have forgotten. And finally, to Kim who has always believed. This is the first, and if it is the last, I hope it is enough.

Photo by Rich Aarstad

Libby Dam from Tony Peak

Preface

Over seventy years ago the residents of the Kootenai Valley had a problem that needed a solution. The Kootenai River wreaked havoc on the lives of those who lived and worked along along its shores, unleashing swirling, savage, silt-laden floodwaters that threatened lives and caused thousands of dollars' worth of damage in its wake. Recognizing the need to control the flooding, the U.S. Army Corps of Engineers proposed a solution; construct a dam of appropriate strength and mass to physically restrain the waters of the Kootenai.

In the process of doing that, the Libby Dam project boldly altered landscapes, disrupted lives, reshaped communities, and overlayed an alternate history of the Kootenai Valley. What follows is a series of vignettes, rather than a chronological narrative, linking the various projects that made up the larger Libby Dam Project, primarily from the perspective of the United States Army Corps of Engineers and a select few who were part of the multi-year/multi-faceted construction project and witnessed the changes it left behind.

For 50 years, the U.S. Army Corps of Engineers has served as stewards of Libby Dam and its environs. The names and faces continue to change as a new generation begins its turn at stewardship. They bring with them adaptations to the dam's operations. One thing remains constant, if sometimes forgotten, the balancing of use with sustainability; never making everyone happy but keeping true to its original mission of flood control and power production.

The following chapters capture only a small slice of the historical narrative that has taken place before and during the construction of Libby Dam. Its shortcomings are many and any errors in historiography, grammar, clarity, and arrangement are mine alone.

Rich Aarstad, Helena, June 21, 2025

August 24, 1975 — President Gerald Ford comes forth to dedicate the dam.

Bold Legacy

Craig Davidson photo

One • The River

Nature is an artist; its brushes and chisels are glaciers, water, and gravity. Not guided by deadlines or caring what critics think, these forces shape, contour, destroy, build up, and level without regard to aesthetics, creating beauties beyond compare. The Kootenai River Valley in northwest Montana is one of these masterpieces. It is in the Kootenai River Valley that this story unfolds regarding the intersection of human settlement, water, and the need for one to harness the power and control the destructive nature of the other.

The Kootenai River is in a remote region far from the beaten path for most. That is not to say that it does not get its share of tourists, but not on the scale of other attractions found under Montana's Big Sky. The river traces its course through an achingly beautiful landscape as it coils its way around mountains and through valleys, passing through the penstocks of Libby

Craig Davidson photo

Dam, over Kootenai Falls, and bending in oxbows near Bonners Ferry, Idaho; where it drifts into the Kootenay Lakes of British Columbia, and from there ultimately passing to the Columbia River and the Pacific Ocean. Flowing through a landscape shaped over millions of years, it courses its way through rock, forest, and towns with an inevitability that is spectacular to contemplate.

Since its discovery and mapping by famed cartographer David Thompson, other travelers pausing along the shores of the Kootenai have commented on

1

its power and grandeur. Author Donald Spritzer related renowned botanist David Douglas' impressions of the Kootenai when he passed through the area in 1827, describing the river as "a stream of considerable magnitude, rapid and very clear."

Another distinguished early visitor to the area, Father Pierre-Jean De Smet, observed the river and all its raw power.

The river is, in this place, deep and tranquil, moving along with a steady pace until aroused from its inertness by the universal thaw; it then descends with such astounding impetuosity that it destroys the banks and in its furious course, uproots and bears along trees, fragments of rocks, and c., which vainly oppose its passage.

The Kootenai provided sustenance to those who chose to make their homes along its banks, but it also reminded them that it was fickle by nature and could take away all they had built in a raging torrent of water.

Photo by Sandy Cmpton

Kootenai Falls, where De Smet waxed poetic, has been recommended as a dam site many times, but the people of Libby thought something upstream of the town would be a "dam sight better."

Two • Floods

The one constant of life along the river involved the apprehension of the spring runoff and wondering if the Kootenai would rise to the occasion, breaching its banks, and laying waste to what lay in its path. To assume escaping flooding in the spring failed to account for the perils of winter, when the river became covered in ice and the cold snap broke, as it often does, with rain that caused the river to thaw and ice jams form. Libby resident Marvin Green recalled when it "…let go, Oh Man! It just tore out the trees along the bank, and it would just raise particular hell. I tell you, that's tremendous power…people just don't have any idea the tremendous power there is in that Kootenai." Green said.

The river unleashed itself upon the communities downstream from Jennings, Montana. with a particular ferocity. The first significant flood on record occurred in 1894, when the waters of the Kootenai tore through the valley with such power and volume that even the steamboats plying between Jennings and Fort Steele, B.C. remained idle that year. Downstream, in Libby, T.L. McCullough recalled

Detail of Ross Hall Photo at Libby Dam Visitor Center

Much of downtown Bonners Ferry was flooded in 1948

3

one of the river's victims was Andy Swann's hotel. The building washed downstream and to the chagrin of Mr. Swann, so did the wall safe that contained his "twenty dollar gold pieces." He rebuilt the hotel downtown, but the fate of the safe remained a mystery.

Twenty-two years later, the river once again breached its banks to embrace with crippling force the communities along its path—a reminder that the Kootenai merely tolerated their presence along its banks. The flood occurred in June of 1916, when warm weather and heavy rains functioned as co-conspirators during the "June rise." The Kootenai's tributaries discharged their snowmelt into the rapidly rising river and the annual purging of the mountain snowpack cut Libby off from the outside world. The flood surpassed the 1894 highwater mark, destroying bridges, homes, and threatening communities from Fernie, B.C. downstream to Bonners Ferry, ID.

Libby Creek breached its banks, cutting a deep channel between the town and the railroad station, complicating efforts to keep the bridge over the Kootenai free of debris. Paul D. Pratt, chairman of the Lincoln County Commissioners and a practical engineer, had a crew throw a temporary bridge over the channel so

work could continue removing debris from around the bridge. When it appeared some of the pylons might give way, Pratt had several dynamite charges placed in the debris wedged in and around the pylons and blasted the threat clear. Then the river receded.

Seventeen years later, in June 1933, a heat wave bumping temperatures into the high nineties spawned a new crisis when the river crested at 15.58 feet above flood stage, surpassing the highwater mark set in 1916. Bonners Ferry once again found itself on the receiving end of the flood waters roiling downstream from Canada and through Montana. Dikes constructed after 1916 to minimize the impact of potential flooding failed, leaving an astonishing 8,783 acres under water. *The Western News* reported that one to two thousand men were working around the clock, and two hundred stranded hoboes joined the ranks in the effort to save the community.

The river did not always flood, but it had a cycle of fifteen to twenty years when it would unleash a particularly destructive torrent downstream, causing unparalleled damage. A month before the 1948 flood season, Lincoln County Commissioners sent a letter requesting assistance from Montana's U.S.

Senators Mike Mansfield and James E. Murray, along with U.S. Representative Zales Ecton, seeking funding for the United States Army Corps of Engineers so that it could continue work on the Flower Creek Flood Control Project. The additional funds would pay to have the channel cleared of debris and stabilize the banks with riprap.

Seattle District Civil Engineer, J.A. Moody, had completed some of the work in April using rented county equipment, clearing twelve hundred feet of creek, while putting in a small levee southeast of Libby and a short dike near the cemetery. Just weeks later, the river became so high that Libby, Flower, and Parmenter Creek flood waters forced the streams back onto themselves, causing residents to evacuate their homes as water came over the banks, and turning Libby into a swamp.

The widespread flooding of the river and its tributaries contaminated the town's water supply when it overflowed sewer systems and septic tanks, spawning the threat of typhoid fever. The effects of the flood were felt the length of the Kootenai River watershed, impacting the Columbia River as well. As residents near and far began cleaning up the debris once again, a consensus was building that perhaps something more than riprap and dikes would be needed to hold the river in check.

Libby's train station during the floods of 1948

Three • Harnessing the Kootenai

The *Western News* reported on a public meeting the U.S. Army Corps of Engineers held at the Dome Theater in Libby on July 1, 1948, to discuss flood control on a larger scale. Addressing a crowd

VOLUME XLVIII

Large Crowd Attends The Dam Hearing Yesterday in Libby

A full house was present at the Dome Theatre yesterday afternoon to hear proposals of the review of the report to be presented to Congress on the proposed Libby Dam which will be constructed, if approved, at a site near Jennings on the Kootenai River.

Presenting plans for the proposed dam before nearly 600 persons were Col. L. H. Hewitt of the U. S. Army Engineers, Seattle and B. P. Thomas, civil engineer from Seattle, who were present at the initial presentation given local people at the Libby courthouse April 17, 1947.

With plans expressed on a much

SOCIAL SECURITY FIELD REPRESENTATIVE COMING

Cecil Cook, Field Representative, Social Security Administration, will be in Libby on Tuesday, July 13, 1948, at the office of the Dept. of Public Welfare from 1:00 to 4:00 p. m., and in Eureka on Wednesday, July 14, 1948 at the office of the Dept. of Public Welfare from 1:00 to 3:00 p. m. He will take applications for benefits under the Federal Old-Age and Survivors Insurance law and conduct other business connected with the federal insurance system.

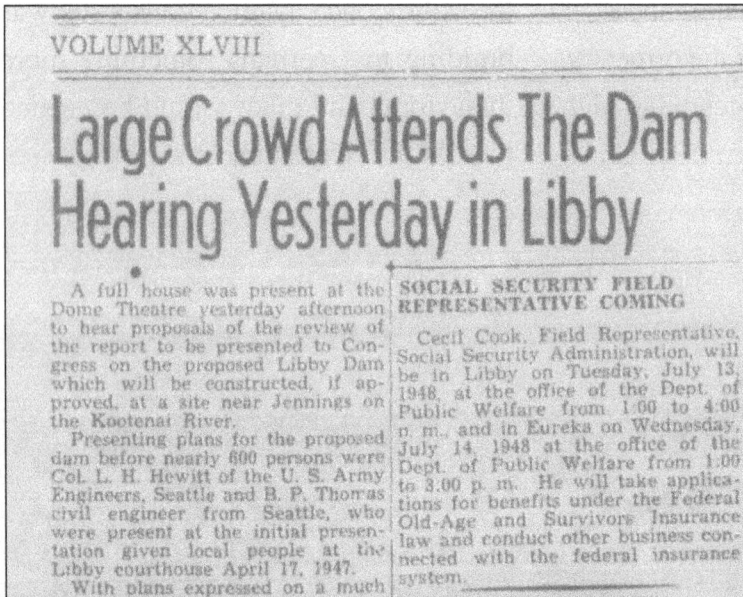

July, 1948, Western News *headline.*

of almost 600 people, Lt. Col. L.H. Hewitt, U.S. Army Engineers, and B.P. Thomas, Seattle District civil engineer, presented proposed plans for a dam on the Kootenai River one and a half miles downstream from Jennings. This

dam would help alleviate flooding and the impounded water would be used to produce hydroelectric power, while an upgraded levee system at Bonners Ferry would guarantee the town's safety. Other benefits mentioned were increased recreation, farm development, and log transportation.

This was not the first time discussion had swirled around the notion of damming the Kootenai. As early as 1912, *The Libby Times* reported army engineers were visiting the river above Kootenai Falls to discuss the placement of a dam at that location. The U.S. House of Representatives Interstate Commerce Committee passed an omnibus dam bill 1912 authorizing companies to construct dams. The Kootenai Power Construction Company received permission to proceed with the construction and operation of a dam around Kootenai Falls for the purposes of navigation. Yet no mention of flood control appeared in the bill or the newspaper reports from that time, however much it was needed. The endeavor ended in 1919 when the federal government cancelled Kootenai Power Construction Company's grant after they failed to raise additional funds from the private sector to finance the project.

The Montana Power Company was next to arrive on the scene in 1917 with the idea of damming the river below the falls, impounding the water and flooding the falls itself. The company estimated the project would cost six million dollars with a two-year completion date. However, with the United States embroiled in World War One and the strike activity at home disrupting the mining and timber industries, it believed construction would have to wait until the labor situation stabilized. However, it never pursued the investment at the conclusion of the war and strike activity.

The major difference between those earlier discussions of damming the river and the proposal being put forward by the US Army Corps of Engineers in 1948 came down to its ability to finance a project of this magnitude. Unlike the private companies before it, the federal government had both deep financial pockets and the expertise to see it completed. However, two significant issues came into focus at that initial meeting in Libby: the cost of compen-

DEVELOP KOOTENAI FALLS

Camps Are Being Constructed at Kootenai Falls for the Use of Surveyors and Engineers. May Change Great Northern Railway Line.

Lumber has been shipped to Kootenai Falls during the past week to be used in the construction of camps for workmen and it is understood that the final surveying and engineering work is to be done at once preparatory to the beginning of actual construction work on the great Kootenai falls power project, which carries with it the establishment of pulp and paper mills and the development of other industries.

The camps will first be occupied by crews of surveyors and civil engineers, about 35 men in all, and will later be used by construction crews, although, of course, larger buildings will have to be put up when the big work starts in order to accommodate all the men, as it is estimated that employment will be given to about 400 workmen when the work is fully under way.

In connection with the development of the falls it may be necessary to nai Falls and Troy, surveys for which have already been made. The building of the big dam, over 100 feet high, makes this advisable, for if the railway line is changed the dam may be built considerably higher than would otherwise be possible.

From all the information that can be obtained everything is looking very favorable for this project and it seems to be certain that it will be pushed through to completion as rapidly as can be ex-

Western News headlines from November, 21, 1912 (above) and October 25, 1917

PLANNING DEVELOPMENT POWER KOOTENAI FALLS

Development of the magnificent power possibilities of the Kootenai falls between Libby and Troy in Lincoln county is about to be undertaken by the Montana Power company, it is said, with the ultimate intention of providing power for the electrification of a stretch of the Great Northern railroad.

Preliminary work for the development of this power was done several years ago by Joseph Coram and associates. The field work has been completed and the office work, such as drafting, etc., is said to have reached a stage where is would be possible to let contracts for construction work.

When completed the power plant on the Kootenai river at the falls will be one of the largest in the state, developing at low water mark, a minimum capacity of 60,000 horse power. With proper care, it is said that 100,000 horse power could be developed.

Plans so far perfected call for a dam across the canyon, below the falls. The water head will be 100 feet. The work will require about two years to complete and will cost approximately $6,000,000. Just

sating the railroad to move its main line and the expense and difficulty of rerouting a significant portion of Montana Highway 37 away from the proposed site of the dam caused some to doubt the feasibility of the proposal. However, since the primary goal of the meeting was fact-finding, Corps of Engineers officials encouraged input from all parties regardless of their stance on the proposed project.

The J. Neils Lumber Company, Libby's largest employer, also had serious concerns regarding the proposed location and put forth the strongest objection to a dam below Jennings. The impoundment would back water up the Fisher River drainage, flooding valuable timberlands recently purchased from the Anaconda Copper Mining Company. As negotiations with Canada occurred and Congress struggled to politic the necessary funds, five years passed and J. Neils hired Montana newspaperman Ernest Immel to write a series of articles for *The Western News* titled, "Libby Dam and Lincoln County's Future." Published between April 2 and May 7, 1953, Immel's articles pointed out the significant loss of income and jobs with the flooding of the lower Fisher River drainage, pointing out that the projected Great Northern Railway relocation would bypass Libby completely.

In response, supporters of the proposed dam touted the economic boon a construction project of this magnitude would bring to Libby, ignoring Immel's arguments as he pointed out the additional cost to the community required to upgrade basic infrastructure and build

U. S. Re-Submits Dam

Sen. Weydemeyer Asks Reelection

State Senator Winton Weydemeyer filed several days ago for reelection on the Republican ticket.

Weydemeyer has served two terms as Lincoln county's senator, during which time he has

Libby Dam Answer To Kootenai Floods

BOISE, May 24—Governor Len Jordan commended federal, state and local officials today for their handling of the Bonners Ferry floods, and said the high water would be a recurring problem "until we get some headwater

Yesterday (May 26) the State Department of Washington re-submitted the Libby Dam to the International Joint Commission, according to a report from Senator Mansfield.

Following is a story telling of difficulties to be overcome before an agreement can become a reality.

OTTAWA—Gen. A. G. L. McNaughton, Canadian chairman of the International Joint Commission, said the United States is abandoning what he called

Headline from The Western News, *May 27, 1954*

larger schools, inflated housing costs, and the inevitable bust that follows every boom — leaving local residents to deal with artificially inflated taxes and a shrinking base to carry that load, as well as the economic losses local business could expect to experience as workers and their families moved on to their next job.

Immel claimed that the primary goal of his series of articles was to awaken the residents of Lincoln County to the indifference federal projects like this paid to the damage done to local economies. Although the initial studies for Libby Dam at that point were already complete, and Congress included the possibility of the construction of the dam in the Flood Control Act of 1950,

Immel hoped that public engagement could still slow and feed the discussion and hopefully lessen the overall impact on the communities along the Kootenai.

The biggest hurdle in the way of the project remained the ongoing negotiations between the United States and Canada, as the construction of the dam would create a reservoir that backed up forty-two miles into Canada. As such, the United States had to shoulder the additional indemnity costs accrued north of the border and determine a fair split of the power generated by the dam. Discussions and bureaucratic red tape would put the project on hold for another fifteen years after Ernest Immel's final article appeared in *The Western News*.

Four • Surveying Into the Future

It is hard to believe that those who proposed the dam could have foreseen a twenty-five plus year lapse between conception and completion. Historian Donald Spritzer attributed this delay as "indicative of the magnitude of the obstacles which had to be surmounted." The primary purpose for the dam's construction remained flood control, as endorsed by the residents of Bonners Ferry, ID and Creston, B.C. The call went out for immediate action but other factors needed addressed: first,

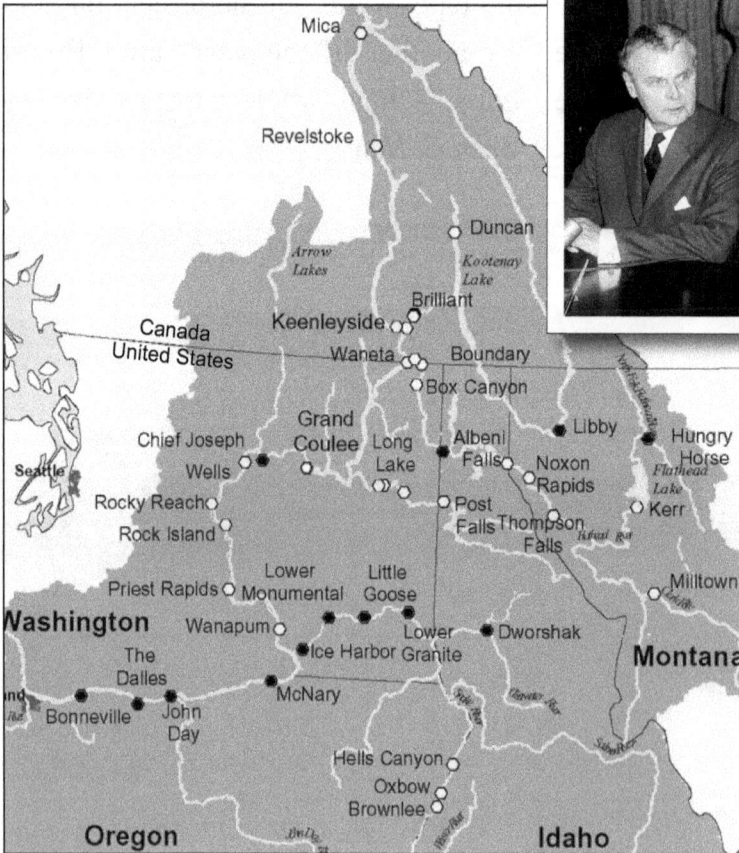

Things began to move quickly after President Eisenhower (right) and Canadian Prime Minister John Deifenbaker signed the Columbia River Treaty.

Dams marked with black dots are US Army Corps of Engineer facilities.

10

U. S. ENGINEERS START WORK ON LIBBY DAM

Full-scale engineering studies have been started on the Libby Dam project and survey teams, drilling equipment and engineers are being mobilized in the area by the U. S. Army Engineer District, Seattle. Thirty men are expected to be in the field this week.

The local press had plenty to report after the signing of the treaty in January of 1961. Above is a headline from the from the April 20, 1961, Sanders County Ledger. *At right is a piece from the August 10, 1961,* Tobacco Valley News.

Prominent Geologist Is Consultant For Army Engineers

One of the nations foremost engineering geologists, Edmond B. Burwell, Jr., has been retained by the U. S. Army Engineer District, Seattle, as a consultant on the Libby dam and reservoir project on the Kootenai River.

He and four Corps of Engineers' men are in Libby and Whitefish area this week for further consid-

more than one hundred and eighteen miles of road needed surveying for the relocation of Highway 37 before construction could even begin; second, sixty miles of the Great Northern Railway needed to be surveyed and laid to re-route the main line, not to mention the construction of a seven mile tunnel through Elk Mountain (the railroad relocation would cost more than the dam construction itself); third, the USACE had to negotiate the land purchases necessary for the project to proceed. Private and government land purchases consisted of over 38,000

acres, to accommodate the impounded water creating Lake Koocanusa.

Long time Lincoln County resident and former county commissioner Jim Morey estimated that about eighty percent of the people in the region were in favor of the dam construction for the promised flood control, the estimated hydroelectric production, and recreational opportunities created by the ninety mile-long reservoir. The remaining twenty percent were those displaced by the creation of the reservoir, purists who wished to see the river remain in its natural state, and anglers who feared the dam would disrupt the natural fishery.

By 1961, their objections were moot. Construction would begin as soon as the site surveys were completed, and the final site selected. Whether Immel's article boosted public engagement or not, one significant difference in the plan from 1948 was the location. Libby Dam would be located above the confluence of the Kootenai and Fisher Rivers, protect-ing valuable timber lands and shifting the Great Northern relocation to an area that traversed part of the original mainline from the 1890s. To address the issue of almost half the new reservoir backing up into British Columbia, the United States and Canada hammered out the Columbia River Treaty, allowing USACE to move forward with the construction at the narrowest point of the river seventeen miles upstream from Libby.[1]

---

[1] The Columbia River Treaty included the construction of four dams, three of them located in British Columbia: Duncan Dam, Mica Dam, and Keenlyside Dam. The United States and Canada reached a tentative agreement in 2024 to renew the treaty that had managed the Columbia River and the hydropower dams on the watershed since 1964. *The Daily Inter-Lake,* 12 July, 2024.

Libby, Montana, Thursday, March 23, 1961   Price 10 Cents

Libby Dam Is Part of River Plan

From Libby's Western News

VOLUME LXXI   KALISPELL, MONTANA, MARCH 23, 1961   NUMBER 37

Libby Dam Planning Money Requested

The movement for an early start of Libby Dam got new momentum when President John F. Kennedy asked Congress to appropriate $350,000 to resume planning. Also the Senate Foreign Relations Committee recommended unanimously that the Columbia River Basin Treaty be ratified. The treaty between the U. S. and Canada, which was signed by President Dwight D. Eisenhower and Prime Minister John Diefenbaker on Jan. 17, governs cooperative development of water resources of the Columbia Basin on both sides of the international boundary. Ratification of the treaty by both nations would remove the final obstacle to construction of Libby Dam on the Kootenai River northeast of here.

At his press conference Kennedy announced he was requesting the $350,000 appropriation to resume planning the Libby project. He asked that the appropriation be included in the supplemental appropriation bill which has already passed the House of Representatives and is now being considered in the Senate.

Sens. Mike Mansfield and Lee Metcalf report that they have dispatched letters and requested to be allowed to appear in person before the Ap-

(Continued on Back Page)

MICK MILLS, J. Neils Lumber Co. photographer, stands on the mountain side overlooking the confluence of Dunn Creek and the Kootenai River and surveys the spot considered most likely for the location of the proposed Libby Dam. Located about 17 road miles northeast of Libby, above the big bend of the Kootenai, the dam here would back water into Canada and provide flood control and power generation facilities.

The photograph accents the magnificent mountain scenery along the Kootenai River which will be flooded by the waters impounded by Libby Dam.

In this photograph, the cameraman is looking northwest. Dunn Creek can be identified by the thin row of trees just to the right of the Kootenai in the center of the picture.

Libby Dam was long ago authorized by the Congress, but international problems have stalled the project.— (J. Neils Photo)—Engraving Courtesy Western News.

In March of 1961, the new President, John F. Kennedy, requested $350,000 to continue preliminary planning and surveys for the dam.

Five • The Resident Engineer

As critical as funding, location, and community support were, choosing the right individual to run the project on the ground was equally important. For this reason, The Seattle District of the USACE would handpick the chief engineer for the Libby Dam project, selecting an individual who had already acquired a reputation for getting difficult projects done and who it believed would be able to manage the daily problems endemic to a project of this magnitude. And while the construction itself had its own headaches, there was also a need to juggle a broad range of responsibilities that went along with the job. The resident engineer's power necessitated being at times part public relations spokesman, part dictator, and part benevolent father figure, and use of it made him an omnipotent figure during the span of the Libby Dam project and its various parts.

Chosen for this position of immense responsibility was Phil Cole, a quiet-spoken man whose acumen as an engineer

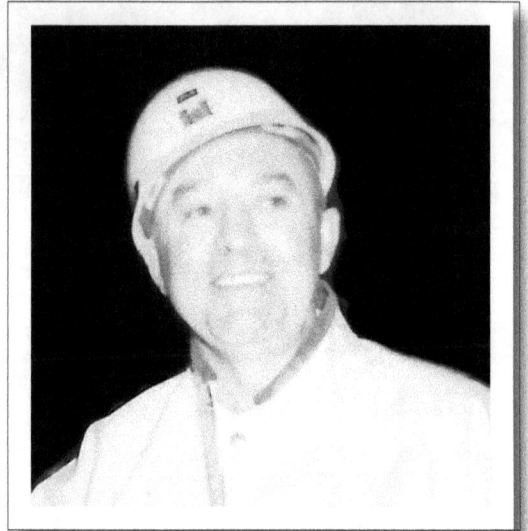

Phil Cole directed the building of Libby Dam, beginning to end. In addition to his engineering skills, he was a master of public relations.

paired nicely with a demonstrated ability to manage people. He was without doubt the right man for the job. Cole arrived in Libby in December 1965, and his first impression of the area was not favorable. The tiny U.S. Forest Service airstrip proved unserviceable, and without improvements would require travel from Seattle to rely on Great Northern passenger service. This was one of the

14

first of many unforeseen problems that required the Corps of Engineers to build a new airstrip and airport to meet their needs. While it proved inconvenient, they managed until the new airport was finished three years later.

Cole's staff consisted of himself and three other Corps employees, who faced a community that had residents who were suspicious of the project, and others who welcomed it with open arms.

Cole had less than a year before the first major milestone for construction needed to occur. Undaunted, he went to work, rising sometimes in the middle of the night to go to the project site and check on the progress. His work ethic was direct; he went to work and worked until there was nothing left to do. His dedication made for long days and short nights on a project that took years to finish. While the various projects associated

15

with the construction of Libby Dam absorbed the majority of Phil Cole's time as resident engineer over the next nine years, he dedicated a portion of his time keeping the public aware of what was going on regarding construction on the dam and the impact it might have on the community. Involvement in the Chamber of Commerce and the Libby Rotary Club

Just one small part of the "boom" mitigation were several new classrooms at Asa Woods elementary school

gave him a venue in which to keep local community leaders and businesspeople abreast of Corps activities. At these meetings he could discuss projected employment for the coming year and alert community leaders when they needed to adjust to the influx of workers and their families. Public schools received constant attention and appropriations of money for the construction of additional buildings, and new schools to accommodate the rapidly expanding student body. This also allowed community leaders to bring in additional teachers, secretaries, librarians, and aides when needed.

More traditional duties took up most of Cole's days. Every contractor had a U.S. Army Corps of Engineers group that worked with them on their particular contract. These groups also insured that the contractor adhered to state and federal prevailing wage laws as applied to federal and service contracts that stipulated wages and benefits must be equal to the prevailing wages of local union and non-union work of the same type. Each contract required thousands of work hours to complete, inspect and approve within a specific length of time. While extensions were possible under extenuating circumstances, they rarely occurred.

Nearly 3,000 Attend

Headline from the August 14, 1966, Independent Record.

Giant Libby Dam Starts, Mansfield Pushes Button

LIBBY (AP) — Sen. Mike Mansfield pushed a button and the boom of exploding dyna- | Observers said the entire hill-side seemed to explode. The principal speakers were | -eration than this project," he said. "What we are beginning today can be of tremendous

Six • Operation B.O.L.D.

The official start of construction seemed like a the perfect time to add a bit of ceremony to the beginning of a project that would impact cities, towns, rural residents in two countries, six states, and one province. It also served international interests by acknowledging the an international agreement between Canada and the United States, The Columbia Treaty of 1961, that took ten years to negotiate. The ceremony was dubbed "Operation B.O.L.D.", Blast off Libby Dam, and required planning to accommodate two thousand vehicles, twenty-six buses, and two special rail cars from Seattle. Invitations went out to eleven hundred dignitaries including U.S. President Lyndon B. Johnson and Canadian Premiere Lester Pearson, along with state and provincial officials instrumental in the negotiations and planning.

U.S. Army Corps of Engineer employees, dignitaries, and interested spectators gathered on an island in the middle of the Kootenai River on August 13, 1966 to watch the blast that would mark the axis of the future dam from one side of the canyon to the other. Operation B.O.L.D. was significant not only because it signaled the beginning of the actual construction of the dam, but also because it began a new era in the valley.

No longer would residents be at the mercy of the raging floodwaters in May and June each year. No longer would the people who owned land on the proposed reservoir site, or who grew up

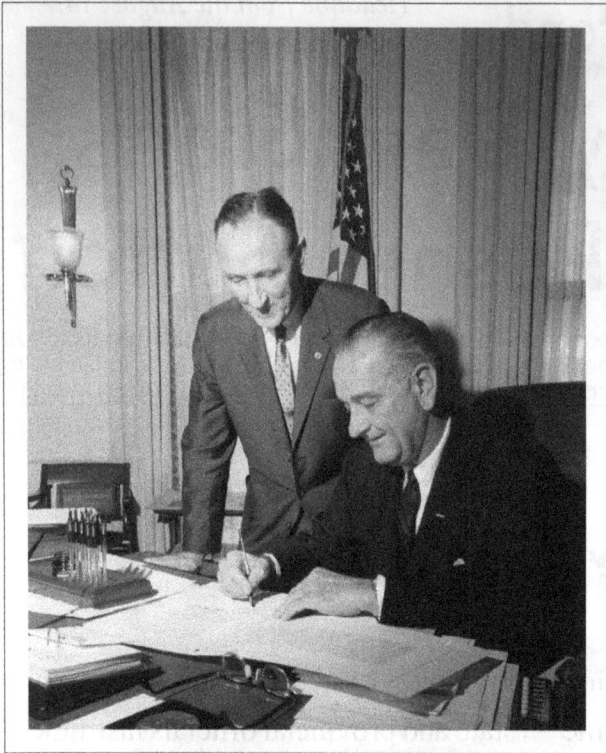

Senator Mansfield (left) pushed the button that began excavation for the dam. President Johnson would set off the charge to "hole through" the Flathead Tunnel via phone.

(Photograph courtesy of the Archives and Special Collections, Mansfield Library, University of Montana.)

tion, recognize the need for larger schools, and reap the benefits of an economy injected with approximately 2,000 new workers. Operation B.O.L.D., therefore, was a beginning and ending in many ways, and the aftershocks of that first blast would reverberate into the future with a resonance that is felt to this day.

As U.S. Senator Mike Mansfield took the stage, he acknowledged the years of debate, dispute, and discord that shook the residents of the Kootenai Valley. He observed that some could never reconcile the loss they suffered or embrace the progress that their sacrifice afforded those down river, but he hoped the generations to come would take advantage of the opportunities provided by the completion of the dam and the harnessing of the power of the Kootenai. Mansfield lauded the project as a "…tremendous benefit to our great state if utilized with care and organization." With that, he turned and pressed the button, and the crowd let out a raucous cheer as the hillside charges exploded.

and lived in the small communities of Warland, Ural, Hayden, and Gateway be able to remain on the land that had been their home. The town of Libby would, at least during construction, boom in a way that the gold prospectors of the nineteenth century had hoped for but never saw. Residents would see firsthand the rapid increase in popula-

Seven • Libby Dam Builders

Big Beginnings at Libby Dam

A new job of dam building is off to a big start on the timber-fringed Kootenai River in northwestern Montana, some 80 miles from Glacier National Park. The project: Libby Dam. Five and a half years of work and more than 3,750,000 cubic yards of concrete will go into this massive, gravity-type structure that will rank among the masonry giants of the world. When finished in 1972, it will loom 420 feet in maximum height. It will shoulder its way across the green waters of the Kootenai to a total crest length of 2,900 feet. It will form a lake, 90 miles long, that will extend 42 miles into neighboring Canada and provide almost 5,000,-000 acre-feet of storage for flood-control and power purposes. Morrison-Knudsen Company, Inc., and four joint-venture associates are building the dam under an $83,000,000 contract that was awarded in mid-March by the Seattle District of the U.S. Army Corps of Engineers. The joint-venture

Morrison-Knudsen announced the project in the October, 1967, eM-Kayan Magazine

Once Operation B.O.L.D. occurred, the next step centered around which construction company's bid would win the bid as the general contractor for Libby Dam. USACE held a pre-bid conference in March 1966 to introduce the various contracts up for bid, including for a general contract to oversee the bulk of the project. Morrison-Knudsen Construction, Perrine Corporation, F&S Construction Company of Butte, Brown & Root Incorporated, and McLaughlin Construction Company of Great Falls attended the conference and the following year, Morrison-Knudsen (functioning as a combine called "Libby Dam Builders") won the bid for the $352 million project.

As the sponsor company, MK combined with Brown and Root, Inc.,

Perini Construction, McLaughlin, In, and F&S Contracting Co., to form the majority of Libby Dam Builders combine, and had just completed Yellowtail Dam on the Big Horn River. Libby Dam Builders officially opened their Libby office in March 1967 having contractually agreed to "…*excavate five million yards of materials, construct the 2,900 foot long, 420 foot high concrete-steel barrier and to begin the storage of water in 2,170 days.*"

Resident Engineer Phil Cole informed *The Western News* that MK would construct approximately six family homes in Libby along with a bachelor camp to house one hundred fifty men near the dam site. Ultimately, the Corps of Engineers issued over one hundred and thirty contracts under the Libby Dam Builders.

Eight • Aggregate

A core sample of the aggregate that composes Libby Dam

Aggregate is a key ingredient of construction, especially construction on the scale of Libby Dam. As the core sample from Libby Dam demonstrates, it took a lot of small pieces, combined, to make the concrete structure spanning the Kootenai River. In a similar vein, it took a lot of different people, aggregate, to place the concrete, relocate the railroad, bore the Flathead Tunnel, construct the Koocanusa Bridge, and much more to put the finish on the Libby Dam Project. From design to naming and honoring the achievement, the following individuals were part of the aggregate that helped bring the project to its conclusion.

The Architect

Paul Thiry's relationship with the U.S. Army Corps of Engineers began several years before he designed Libby Dam. Thiry had designed several buildings for the Corps and in 1952 reviewed the architectural drawings for the Chief Joseph Dam powerhouse and other architectural features of the Chief Joseph

Wikipedia Commons

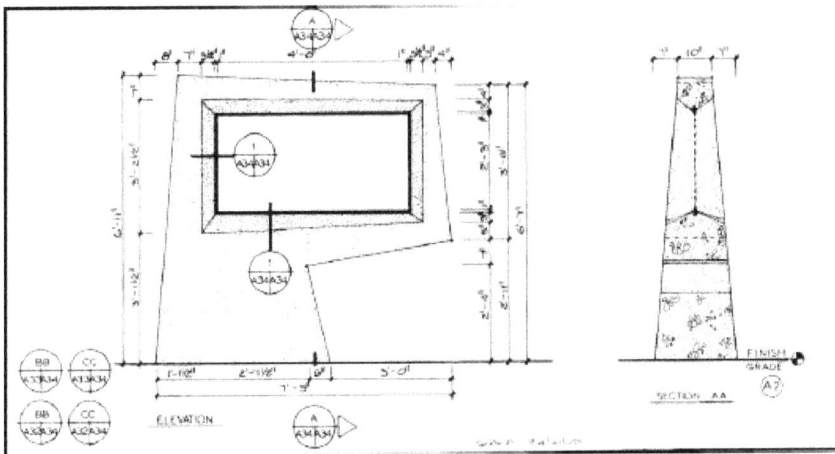

Location:	Design features						
Treaty Tower	sculpture						
Visitor Center	Angled roof	Massive pillars	No square corners	Clerestory lights	handrails	Drinking fountain on roof	Exposed concrete
Dam	Angled surfaces		No square corners				
Powerhouse	Angled Surfaces	t-frames	No Square Corners				

Thiry's design incorporated lots of exposed concrete, but no square corners.

The display case in the powerhouse (right) is a good example of his work.

Dam project. Ten years later Sydney Steinborn, chief of the Seattle District Engineering Division, called Thiry up and asked if he would be interested in consulting on the entire project, "not just the fussy-dussy part of it."

As an environmentalist, Thiry seemed a strange choice for a dam project, but the Corps of Engineers saw the benefit of engaging someone of Thiry's reputation for two reasons. First, his design

would demonstrate the Corps' frugal and discriminating use of taxpayer dollars and second, the design of the dam and surrounding structures would draw

21

in tourists to see firsthand how hydroelectric power worked in tandem with flood control for the benefit of the greatest number of people. Thiry's vision embraced the inclusion of a museum, guided tours, lectures, and features designed to increase recreation.

In the process, Thiry and his team created approximately ten different schemes for Libby Dam, always adjusting and tweaking the design to find ways to create interest and accommodate the public. He sought to create a design that would carry through to every feature of the dam, surrounding administrative structures, the powerhouse, and recreational areas; always monolithic, blended, and merging into the natural setting.

Paul Thiry, who became known as the "father of Northwest Modernism," favored massive concrete designs with "no square corners." This is apparent in the design of the Libby Dam Visitors Center, with its sloped roof, exposed concrete walls inside and out, and unique lighting system.

Lady Koocanusa

Alice M. Beer was mad! Fighting mad, and she would countenance no nonsense from the editor of the *Helena Independent Record*. "Just finished reading your 15-year-old 'Hippies' smart remarks regarding Arnold Olsen's submission of a bill in Congress to name the new lake behind Libby Dam as Koocanusa." This was not her first time brawling over the right of Lincoln County residents to name their new lake. Ever since she had suggested the name—combining the first three letters of Kootenai with the first three letters of Canada, and

Koocanusa Group Pushes Letter Writing Campaign

A joint Canadian-American letter writing effort to get the waters impounded behind Libby Dam named Koocanusa has been started by the Lake Koocanusa Naming Group, according to Alice M. Beer, secretary.

The Koocanusa name is a coined word combining Kootenai (koo) from the river upon which the dam is being constructed, (Canada (can) and United States of America (usa) since the waters backed up by the dam will be in both countries.

Sens. Mike Mansfield and Lee Metcalf and Congressmen Arnold Olsen and James Battin. The letters can be sent to each of the men in care of the U.S. Senate or House of Representatives, Washington, D.C.

Canadians are asked to write Premier W. A. C. Bennett, Premier of British Columbia, House of Parliament, Victoria, B.C.; Leo T. Nimsick, M.L.A., Kootenay East, B.C., House of Parliament, Victoria; and James A. Byrne, Kootenay East, B.C.,

Above: From the October 20, 1968,
Daily Inter-Lake.

Lower right: September 28, 1969. Great Falls Tribune

letter writing campaign by Canadian and American supporters alike.

The second hurdle emerged from J. O. Kilmartin, executive secretary of the U.S. Board on Geographic Names in Washington, D.C. He declared that "where a proposed name involves a feature associated with a Corps of Engineers project, the board. . .[seeks] the opinion of the Corps" on whether the authorizing legislation had already established a name. In a wise political move, the Corps deflected,

then adding U.S.A. to create the name KooCanUsa—it seemed an uphill battle.

The first hurdle came in 1967, when the East Kootenay Historical Society in British Columbia suggested the name Lac Morigeau after Francois Morigeau, a French voyageur and missionary who explored southern Alberta, British Columbia, and Montana in 1819. With half of the reservoir located north of the border, it seemed to them that they had as much a right as the Americans to name the new lake. While the Morigeau name resonated with the Canadians and had some familiarity south of the border, it did not sing. As such, the Rexford committee traveled north to make their case for Koocanusa, and in 1968 the Canadian Committee on Geographical Names gave its approval after a vigorous

Metcalf Reintroduces Bill To Name Libby Dam Lake

By Tribune Correspondent

EUREKA — Sen. Lee Metcalf has introduced a bill to designate the lake to be formed by waters impounded by Libby Dam as "Lake Koocanusa." A previous bill during the last session died for lack of action.

Mrs. Alice M. Beer of Rexford received notice that the bill S2870 had been reintroduced, and that petitions received by the Board on Geographic Names regarding the naming of the lake, had been placed on file, according to Sen. Metcalf.

She also received a second letter from Rep. Arnold Olsen enclosing the State Department Review of the proposed name "Lake Koocanusa." Olsen stated "I am most enthusiastic that all people concerned support this name and applaud you and your group for your fine efforts."

The Department of State letter reports that there is no objection to the proposed bill, and that the department has ad-

vised informally by the Canadian Embassy that the government of Canada intends to adopt that name. The letter was signed by John P. White, acting assistant secretary for congressional relations.

Koocanusa Clears Another Hurdle

EUREKA — Congressman Arnold Olsen reports that another hurdle has been crossed in the efforts to have the name "Koocanusa" approved for the reservoir to be formed by Libby Dam on the Kootenai River in Northwestern Montana. "I have just been notified that the Canadian Permanent Committee on Geographical Names has given its approval to the name," reports Olsen.

The new name combines the names Kootenai, Canada and USA. "I am hopeful the Congress

Above: From the August 5, 1968, Daily Inter-Lake.

Below: Victory! Through persistence and aided by international cooperation, Alice Beer had her way. From the January 15, 1970, Missoulian.

House Passes 'Lake Koocanusa' Title for Libby

WASHINGTON, D. C. (AP) — In what Rep. Arnold Olsen, D-Mont., called a "victory of local interests over bureaucracy," the House of Representatives Thursday passed legislation naming the reservoir behind Libby Dam "Lake Koocanusa."

claiming that the name could only come by legislative action. As such Senator Lee Metcalf, of Montana, introduced S2870 to name the reservoir Lake Koocanusa, while Representative Arnold Olsen lobbied the U.S. Department of State to offer no objection to the bill. At this point, the final hurdle came from Montana's capital city newspaper, The *Helena Independent Record*.

The *Helena IR* editor, who did not sign his jibe at the Koocanusa name, seemed to find the entire process amusing and worthy of vulgar jest. The editor callously clarified that, no, it was not the name of an Indian prostitute banished to the area because everyone knew only Coast Guard cutters were named after Indian prosti-

tutes. He then questioned the order of the letters suggesting Usacankoot, or Canusakoot, or Cankoosa as candidates. His attempt at humor was uncouth, insulting, and laced with racism, and Beer and her allies were having none of it.

Beer defended the name and its Indian connotation, pointing out that it fit with other place names in the area such as Kasanka River and Tobacco Plains. She also called out the editor's obscene and racist remarks, pointing out "we respect, far more than you, our aborigine, the American Indian." Richard C. Shirley, editor of the *Tobacco Valley News*, weighed in as well, suggesting the Helena editor "had better keep a civil tongue in regards to this matter, as the name is pretty well accepted here whether it becomes official or not." In 1970, Beer and the members of the Koocanusa naming group celebrated their victory when Congress officially approved the name Koocanusa for the reservoir.

In recognition of her efforts, Alice Beer acquired the title of Lady Koocanusa, in 1973. By this time, she was spending a considerable amount of time in and out of the Kalispell hospital. She died at age 79 in May 1975, just months before the Libby Dam's final dedication.

The Treaty Tower

The tower atop Libby Dam in northwestern Montana is truly representative of the International Treaty between Canada and the United States. The upstream face of the tower contains a massive sculpture piece commemorating the agreement between the two countries for the cooperative development of the vast Columbia River Basin water resources.

The concept of a "Treaty Tower" with a sculptured face was developed with Seattle architect Paul Thiry, Architectural Consultant for the Libby Dam Project, to add visual and aesthetic impact to the engineering concepts of the dam. Thiry1s proposal was incorporated into the final plans and in 1972 the Seattle District of the Army Corps of Engineers, designers and builders of the dam, set about selecting a sculptor for the job.

To do this, the Corps staged an international competition. After a two-stage contest, Albert Wein, well-known sculptor from Encino, California, was named the winner, Wein received first prize of $15,000 and the opportunity to negotiate a contract with the Corps of Engineers for professional services in the production of the sculpture.

Wein's winning design features an Indian restraining two rearing horses, symbolizing the harnessing of natural forces by man. Clouds, rain, geese in flight, leaping fish, and water are combined to stress the ecological aspects of

Bold Legacy

the project. Near the bottom of the design, an eagle and a maple leaf signify the international cooperation necessary to bring the huge dam project to fruition.

Gray granite from the "Granite Capitol of the World" — Barre, Vermont — was chosen. The Rock of Ages quarry supplied the nine slabs of granite, each weighing ten tons. Near the quarry, Wein, on hand for the entire production process, directed two master carvers in their work. The giant basrelief sculpture measuring, 27 by 30 feet when assembled, was carved from a one-third size plaster model. During the carving process about fifteen tons of stone were reduced to chips by the carvers as they wielded pneumatic hand chisels.

Installation of the 75-ton sculpture was complete in time for the August 24, 1975 dedication ceremonies.

The scale of the sulpture is demonstrated by contrast with the sculptor Wein, standing in the center (above right).

At right, the sculpture is being mounted to the face of the tower atop the dam.

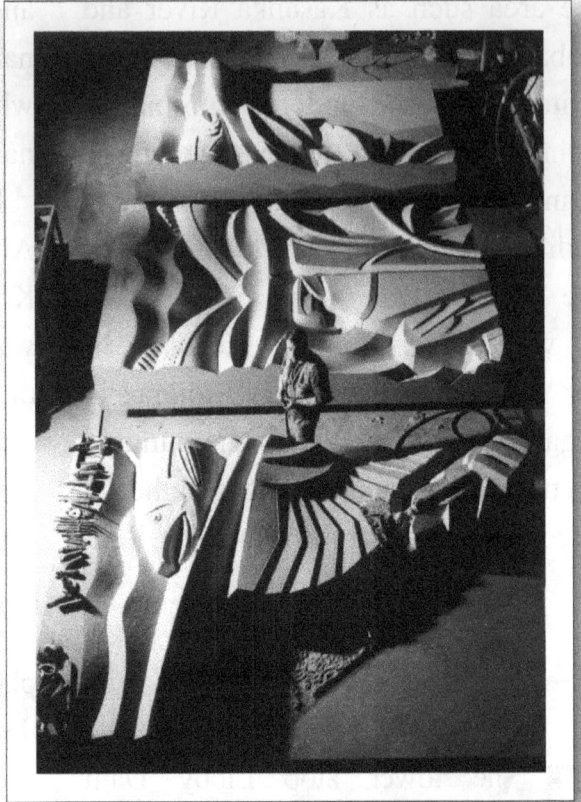

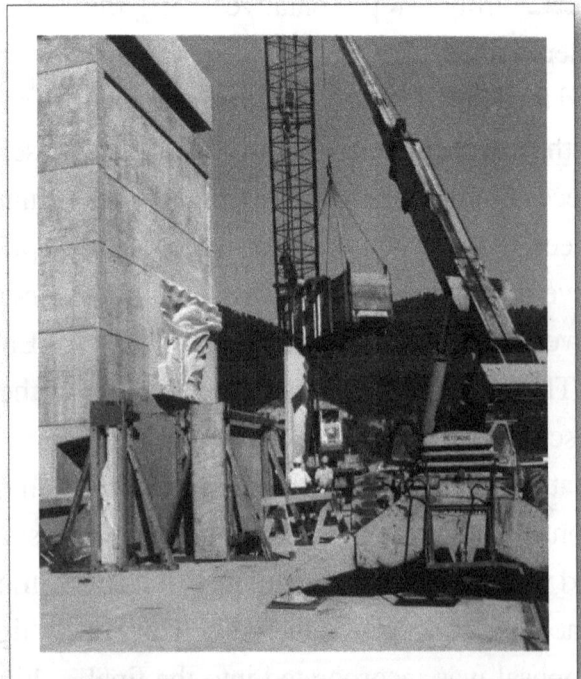

26

Nine • Milestones

Holing Through on the Flathead Tunnel

Cole took every available opportunity to get the project in the media to commemorate major milestones of construction progress. The first major public relations event took place two years after operation B.O.L.D. Working from both sides of Elk Mountain, the scheduled holing through of railroad tunnel was set for June 21, 1968. President Lyndon B. Johnson would push a button from the Oval Office in Washington D.C. sending a signal through the telephone lines detonating the charges in Montana. Cole, as an engineer, never left anything to chance and set up a redundancy system that ensured success.

Not trusting the telephone line connection from Trego, after President Johnson pressed the but-

Above: Humble beginnings of a monumental project. Right: The result of President Johnson's button pushing.

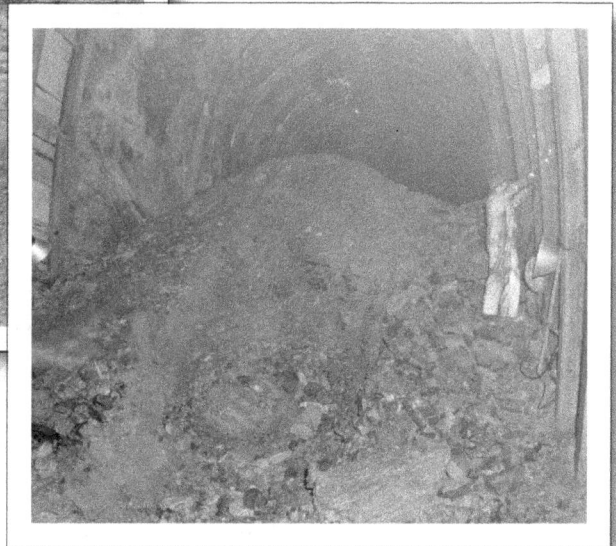

ton, one of his men announced the act and a man on site simultaneously pressed the button on a backup detonator just in case. When questioned by a reporter which button detonated the charge, Mr. Cole replied with confidence "President Johnson's." Work on the tunnel included the installation of a massive exhaust system to flush toxic diesel fumes from it as trains passed through.

In the age of air travel and automobiles, people tend to forget the importance of the Great Northern's transcontinental rail line though the Kootenai Valley. It played a vital role in the lives of the people who lived along the upper Kootenai, providing jobs and transportation, while delivering merchandise from around the world. It provided economic stability and a sense of permanence. Relocating the main line would leave Rexford and Eureka with limited access and contact with outside interests.

The relocation of the Great Northern Railway line alone cost over seventy million dollars. It also dictated the pace of dam and Highway 37 construction as progress on both adjusted their timeline to meet the needs of the Great Northern as its uninterrupted operation remained the priority until the new mainline was completed. A gap was left on the east side of the river for the railroad tracks and scheduled trains rumbled through the middle of the dam construction on a regular basis. With the imminent approach of its completion by early November 1970, it seemed appropriate to celebrate this major milestone.

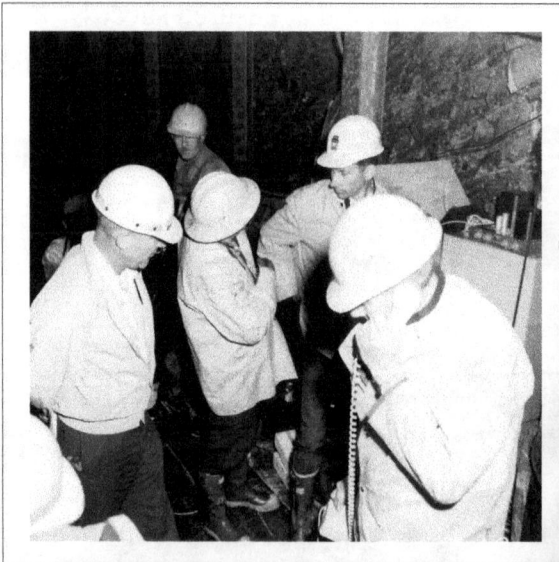

Above: Project manager Phil Cole on the phone with President Johnson.
Right: Cole congratulates tunnel project manager Les Huntington.

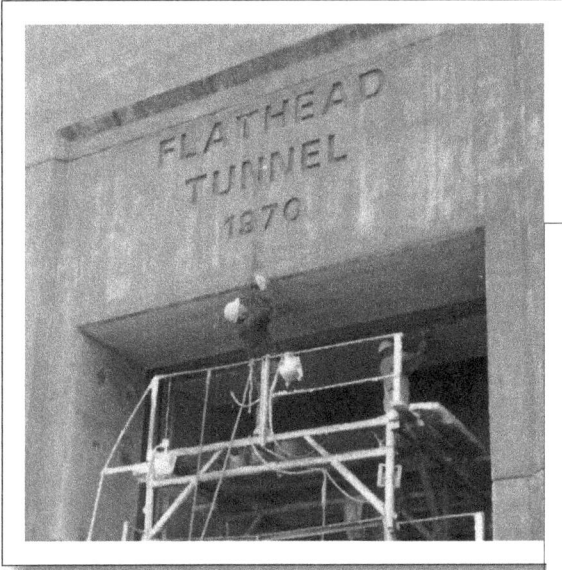

Left: Finishing touches on the west portal of the Flathead Tunnel.

Below: This huge batch plant provided the concrete for the tunnel.

First Train Ceremony

The Army Corps of Engineers, Great Northern/Burlington Northern Railroad[1], and the Libby Chamber of Commerce sponsored the First Train Ceremony for November 7, 1970. A special train would leave the Libby depot and travel over the recently completed fifty-nine mile-long railroad line between Jennings and Stryker. The train would consist of twenty-one cars carrying approximately 1,100 people. Once the train reached Stryker, it would proceed up the old line to Eureka and Rexford, then back down the Kootenai River Valley through the railroad adit in Libby Dam and return to Libby. In a sense, the "First" Train Ceremony was also the

[1] The Great Northern and Burlington Northern had merged the previous year, but for clarity's sake, the author will continue to use the Great Northern name.

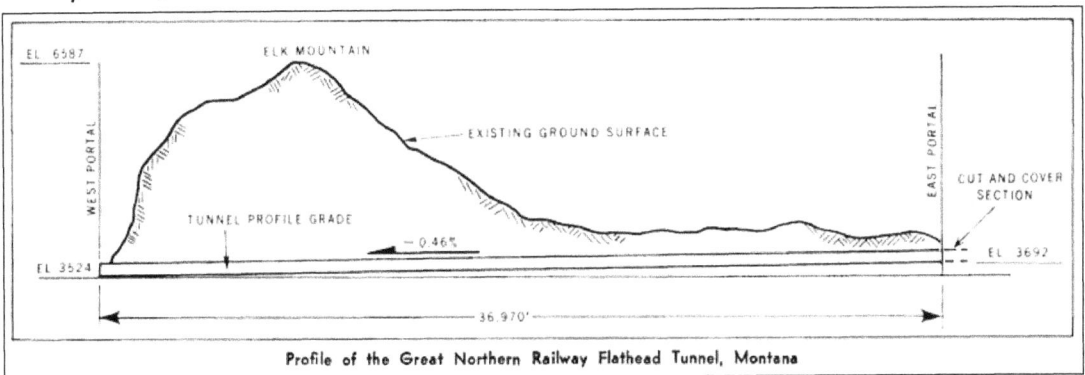

Profile of the Great Northern Railway Flathead Tunnel, Montana

Bold Legacy

"Last" Train Ceremony for the old line that had been in operation since 1904. The railroad, recognizing the historical significance of the train ride, along with the Libby Chamber of Commerce sold tickets for $1.50 apiece, first come first serve. The train ride sold out several weeks before the scheduled event was to take place.

Before the train departed Libby, obligatory speeches were made to the passengers and interested bystanders. The first to speak was Colonel H.L. Sargent, Jr., Seattle District Commander:

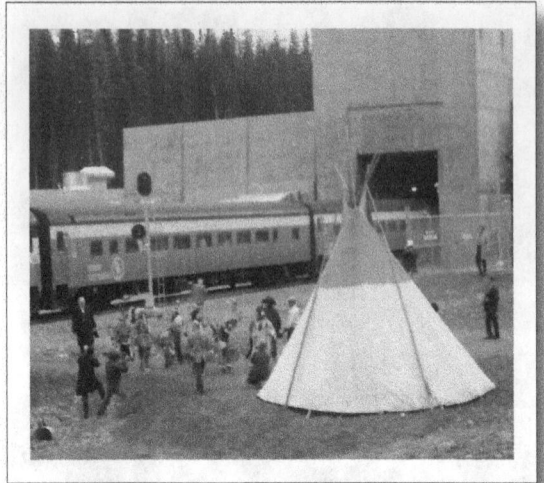

The Kootenai Tribe helped celebrate the first train through the tunnel.

You will go through the second longest railroad tunnel in the western hemisphere . . . you will not be able to see daylight from one end of the tunnel to the other because of the curvature of the earth . . . this tunnel is an engineering marvel. It was excavated from both ends simultaneously utilizing laser beams to assure accurate alignment . . . when you work both ends against the middle you usually end up in trouble, when the crews working from opposite ends of the tunnel met, their alignments were less than three inches apart and this tunnel is seven miles long.[2]

With that John A. Beyer, regional vice president for Morrison-Knudsen, rose to speak for all the contractors involved in the railroad relocation. He started off by thanking the town of Libby for letting

them "borrow" Mayor Earle Winfrey, who served as the safety supervisor during the track and signal installation. More than three hundred and fifty men put in 450,000 man-hours on the relocation job with only a few minor accidents.

Referencing the turmoil of the times, Mr. Beyer commented to the large gathering at the Libby train station,

---

[2] *The Western News,* Libby, MT, 12 November 1970.

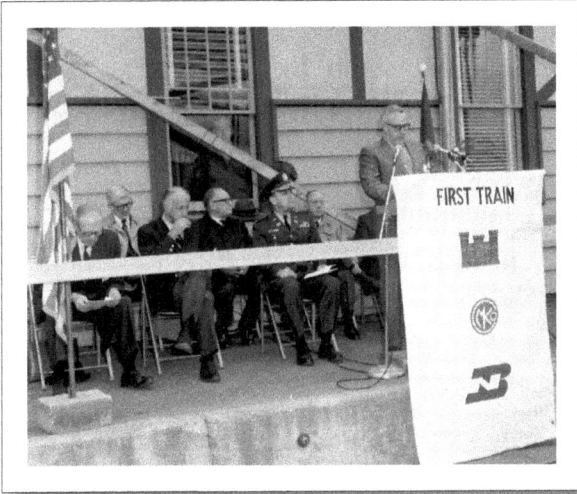

Worthington Smith of Great Northern was one of many speakers at the first train cermony.

"large groups are looked upon as mobs and mobs are to be feared. You are not a mob and you are not to be feared, but you are to be congratulated. You are to be congratulated because you are here to recognize building up and positive accomplishment."[3]

Cooperation between private and government spheres had come together to accomplish a goal and succeeded in completing one of the key elements to the completion of Libby Dam.

Continuing along this vein, John M. Budd, chairman of the board of the Great Northern pointed out "any accolades . . . would be hollow without recognizing

the men, who through their physical efforts, translated plans and ideas into actual cuts, fills, ballast, tracks and a seven-mile tunnel through the mountains." By working together great accomplishments were being made that would benefit those who had been at the mercy of the Kootenai River during the dreaded May and June rises.

With the completion of the speeches, a banner-breaking ceremony took place at Jennings as the special train started up the new route. The new line traversed the "more favorable portion of the original line, following Wolf Creek and the Fisher River," according to Budd. The original route had been "abandoned in 1903 in favor of the line down the Tobacco and Kootenai Rivers," and now it was returning to reclaim part of its historic route with a new twist: instead of going over the mountain it was going through.

For safety purposes, John Coyle, an engineer for USACE, traveled several miles in front of the train to ensure its safe passage. The train maintained a forty-mile per hour speed on the new rail-

---

[3] The turbulence of the 1960s and 1970s — freedom marches opposing discrimination against African Americans, demonstrations against U.S. involvement in the Vietnam War, the assassinations of President John Kennedy, civil rights leader Martin Luther King, Jr. and Senator Robert Kennedy — gave testimony to the rising tide of public discontent. Any group gathering during these years drew suspicion in case violence erupted.

road line and twenty-five mile an hour speed limit through the tunnel. At the north end of the tunnel a small ceremony commemorated its passage through the mountain. Once it reached Stryker, the train turned north on the old line and proceeded to Eureka and then Rexford. Turning south the passengers viewed firsthand the clearing of the river bottom in preparation for the future reservoir. The train returned to Libby at 6:30 p.m. having completed the trip in five hours.

President Nixon and The Three Millionth Cubic Yard of Concrete

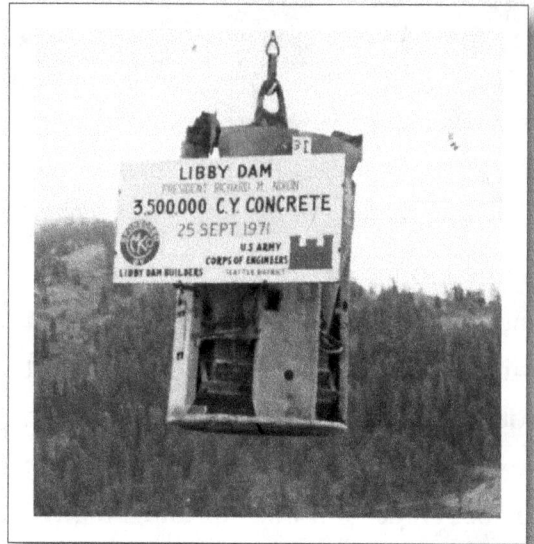

The bucket was full of the real stuff, causing a delay in its delivery.

One of the more famous, or infamous depending on who told the story, events happened in 1971 when President Richard Nixon along with First Lady Pat Nixon decided to visit the construction project, accompanied by U.S. Senator Mike Mansfield and wife Maureen as well as U.S. Representative Richard Shoup and his wife Marjorie. Phil Cole saw an opportunity for more positive press coverage by having President Nixon "bust" the three millionth cubic yard of concrete poured to date in the dam construction.

Cole, understanding these events never occurred on time, gave very specific instructions that he wanted only sand and aggregate in the bucket. He wanted to avoid any chance of embarrassment if President Nixon pulled the lanyard and the load of concrete failed to drop. The contractor's crew would just have to shovel out the fake load later. Unbeknownst to him, USACE employee Tony Munch and the contractor decided to go ahead and dump a real load. Their strategy was simple; they put only ice in the mixture, so if the ceremony ran long, the mix would stay liquid and drop normally, saving the work crews some strenuous shovel work.

President Nixon and enteourage were three hours late for the "bucket busting."

Unfortunately for them, the ceremony started hours late as Cole had anticipated and when it came time for President Nixon to dump the bucket, time was already working against a successful operation. President Nixon took the lanyard in hand and gave it a sturdy tug, putting more effort into it than was necessary since the lanyard only tripped the lever that released the bucket by steam/hydraulic power. Nothing happened. The President pulled harder, but still nothing. Cole began to smell a rat and signaled to one of his men to put a vibrator over the edge of the bucket to help jar the load loose.

President Nixon, refusing to admit defeat, exhorted Senator Mansfield and Representative Shoup to join him on the lanyard. The symbolism of Democrats and Republicans working hand in hand together was too good of a photo opportunity to miss.[4] Three vibrators later and after much effort on the part of three men on the line, the bucket opened and the concrete fell into place. President Nixon seemed extremely pleased with everyone's efforts congratulating the two Montana Congressmen for their assistance and left a happy man. Later Cole called Tony Munch into his office and quizzed him on what happened. When Munch admitted to ignoring his boss's instructions Cole stated that Munch came "extremely close to having to find new employment."

---

[4] A photograph of the three men pulling together on the lanyard hangs in the Libby Dam Visitors' Center showing their effort and resolve while Resident Engineer Phil Cole stares with a slight smile in the direction of the recalcitrant bucket of concrete.

Koocanusa Bridge

Construction on the bridge began in 1967 and cost nine million dollars. Prime contractors R.A. Heintz and Willamette-Western Corporation lauded the fact that not one lost-time accident occurred on the project. Morrison-Maierle, Inc. of Helena designed the bridge. Each concrete pier soared to the height of a twenty-five story building and contained twenty-two thousand cubic yards of concrete, reinforced with one thousand nine hundred tons of steel.

Upon completion, the 2,437 feet long and 290 feet Koocanusa Bridge became Montana's longest and tallest bridge. Located 34 miles above Libby Dam it connects Highway 37, on the east side of the reservoir, with the Forest Service Development Road and the small settlement of West Kootenai. At full pool, the bridge sits seventy-five feet above the reservoir.

Aerial view of four bridge piers in place.

Montana's longest, tallest bridge has most of its height under Lake Koocanusa.

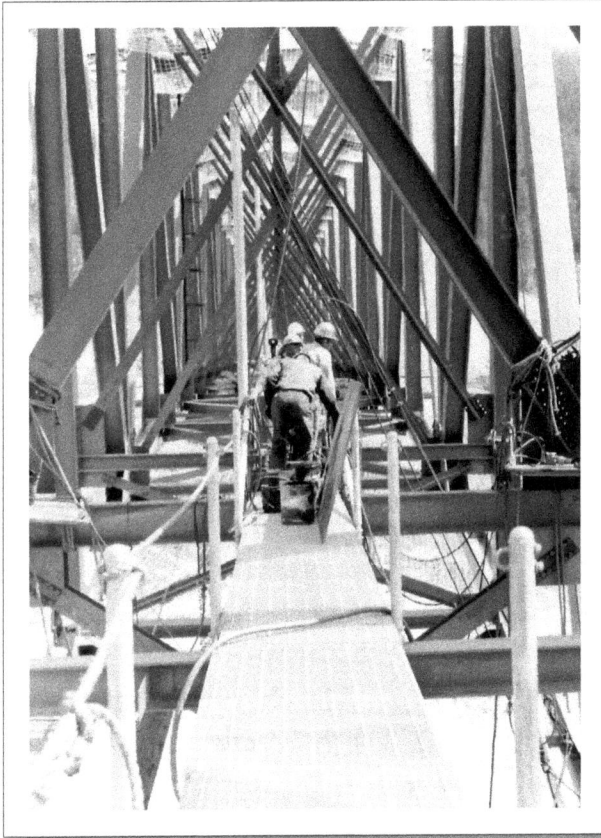

The girder-style bridge is nearly a half mile long, cost 9 million dollars and took thousands of man hours.

Montana Attorney General Robert Woodahl addressed over six hundred people at the ceremony:

This dedication provides an opportunity to reflect upon the cooperative efforts of sovereign nations. This bridge as an integral part of the total project (Libby Dam Project) stands as a reminder of what can be accomplished when nations pool their resources to achieve a common goal....This project we dedicate today stands as a perpetual symbol of this cooperative spirit between these nations.[5]

When the ribbon dropped, Resident Engineer Phil Cole, driving the dignitaries, led one hundred and fifty vehicles over the bridge.

---

[5] *The Daily Inter Lake*, 07 November 1971, page 1.

Ten • A Photographic Progression

June of 1966: *ground clearing for railroad relocation begins.*

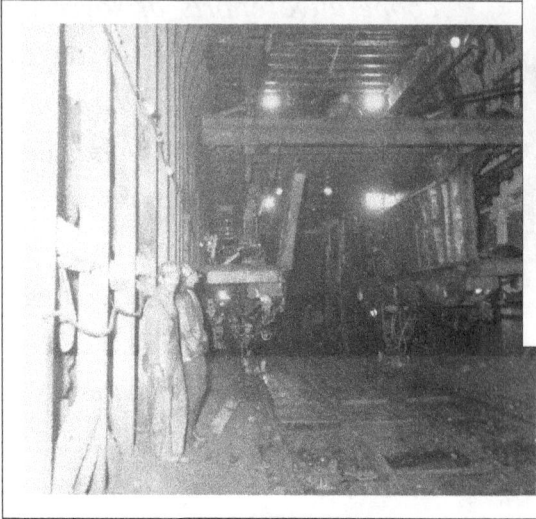

March, 1968: *(below) The "whirly" crane trestle is begun.*

March, 1967: *(above) The west portal of the 7-mile Flathead Tunnel.*

June, 1968: *(below) The first bucket of cement hits bedrock.*

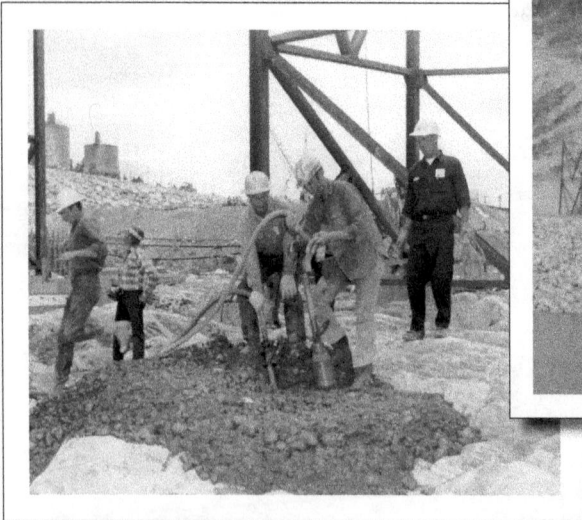

September 1968: *The base of the dam is being established on bedrock .*

Summer 1969: *Night shifts were made possible by the Starlight system.*

July 1969: *Scaling bedrock was difficult, dangerous work.*

September, 1969: *The "whirly" crane trestle is complete.*

Bold Legacy

June, 1970:

At right: Two million cubic yards and counting.

Below: Relocation of buildings in preparation for reservoir flooding begins.

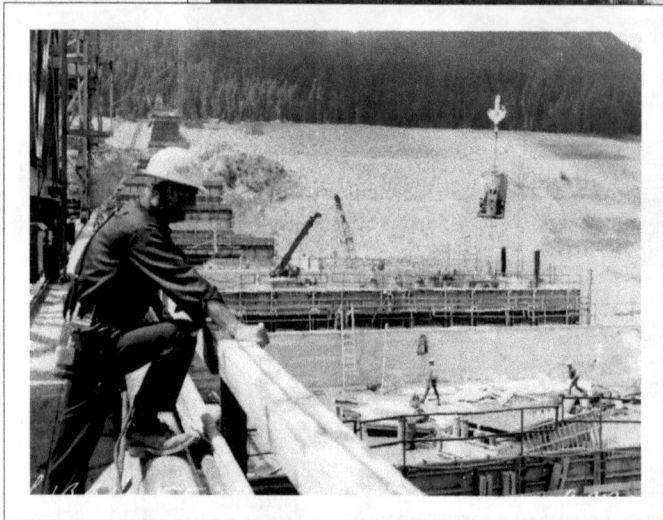

May, 1971:

Above: The face of the dam is well-defined.

At left: Concrete superintendent Jack Burrows keeps an eye on progress

May, 1971: *(at left) Working to secure the Dirty Shame slide face.*

August 1971: *(below) Reservoir clearing is nearly complete.*

Photo by Harold Carbine

Photo by Harold Carbine

January 1972:

Above: *Snow clings to the face of the dam.*

At right: *Winter doesn't stop construction work.*

1973

January: (at left) The face of the dam is complete.

July: (below) Construction has begun on the powerhouse.

August 24, 1975: *(At left)President Gerald Ford greets the crowd at the dam's dedication.*

1986: *(below) The completed dam,*

A couple of thousand men and women — and at least one dog — worked at putting Libby Dam together.

Eleven • Voices From the Past

John Coyle – Assistant to the Resident Engineer

Since the United States Army Corps of Engineers was responsible for Libby Dam's construction, it seems only natural that some members of the United States Army would be assigned to the project. First Lieutenant John Coyle was one of these individuals. Lieutenant Coyle was in Vietnam in 1970 when he was offered a job a working on the dam. He called his wife, Mary, back in the United States, getting her out of bed to ask her

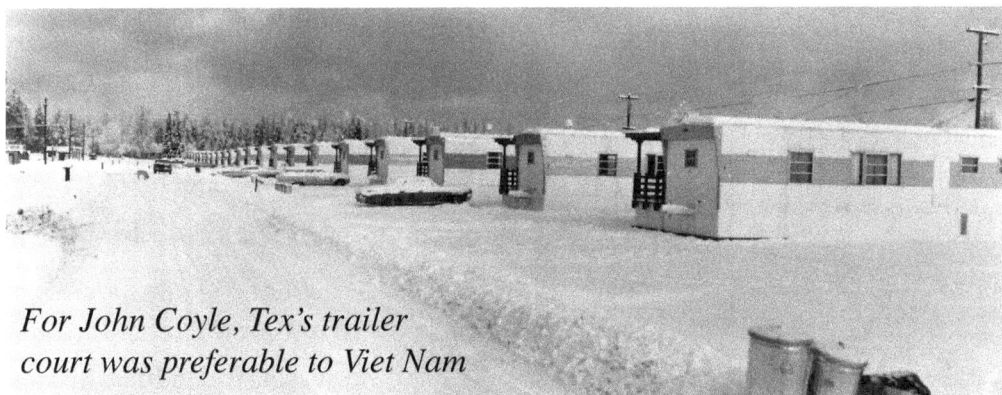

For John Coyle, Tex's trailer court was preferable to Viet Nam

41

advice, and she told him to do what he thought was best. Scrounging around, he found a tattered copy of an atlas and looked for Libby on the map. When he found it, it only showed one road into the town; he accepted the job. When he and Mary arrived, he admitted they experienced some culture shock, but it quickly faded as they made themselves at home in a government trailer in "Tex" Reese's Trailer Court. They made the acquaintance of other families and decided, "Libby was a pretty nice place to be with all the recreation opportunities."

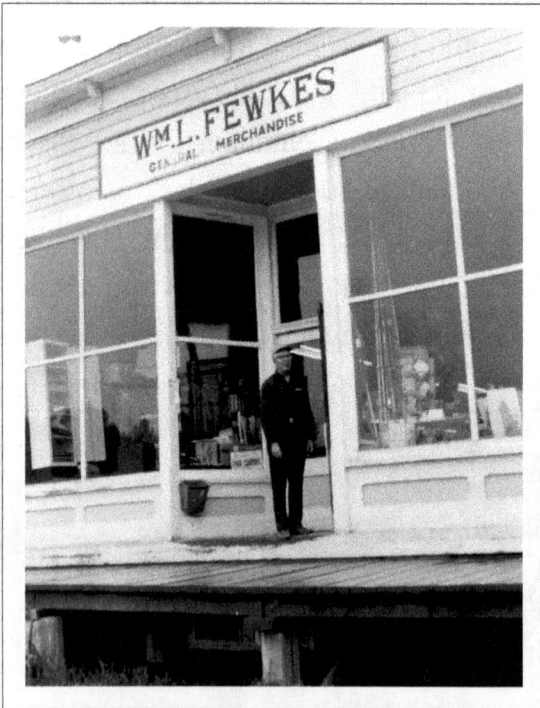

Fewkes' Store, where the peanuts were purchased, was relocated.

Coyle was assigned as an assistant to the resident engineer and with his forestry degree he was put to work on the reservoir-clearing project, which had already started. Other military personnel were also assigned to the Libby project; they included Chad Cox, Ernie Schrader, and Paul Reigh. The idea was to get these men training and experience on large projects for the time when they would get their own commands of districts within the Corps of Engineers.

Upon his arrival, Coyle soon earned the nickname Captain Crunch for frequently getting his pickup truck stuck or high centered as he cruised the timber clearing project. This tendency to require assistance led to his introduction to Miles Briggs, a Libby native working in the USACE motor pool and maintenance department.

In one incident, Coyle accidentally backed into an old septic tank at the Warland town site. Briggs responded to the distress call and pulled Coyle out of the "stuff," marking the start of a long career for Miles, pulling Coyle out of, over, and through rough spots on the road above Libby Dam. Clearing of the reservoir proved one of many memorable events for Coyle, as the land was stripped bare in preparation for flooding the river valley.

One project that Coyle worked on was the railroad salvage job. He and Sally Price, a coworker, spent quite a bit of time traversing the old railroad line in conjunction with their other duties ensuring the rails, spikes, ties, and tie plates were removed. One of their favorite places to stop was Bill Fewkes' store in Rexford. They would purchase a bag of peanuts, still in the shell, and munch on them for the rest of the day, discarding the shell fragments on the floor of the vehicle they were driving. Later that day when they returned to the motor pool they laughed in delight at the look of consternation on the face of Miles Briggs as they opened the doors and the peanut shells fell out.

In fascination, Coyle watched as the forty-seven individual monoliths that comprised the bulk of the dam staggered upward and marveled at the alignment of the drainage and grouting galleries as the monoliths stair-stepped to completion. He was promoted to Captain in the United States Army Reserve but decided not to pursue a regular army commission. He left the service in 1973 and returned to Libby that same year as a civilian employee of the Corps of Engineers. He was assigned as resource manager for the project to help coordinate the changeover from construction to operation and maintenance of the facility.

Like most Corps employees he oversaw more than one facet of the construction phase. One of his duties was drift control. A log boom was attached from one side of the reservoir to the other just above the dam. The boom was of sufficient length that it would stretch and contract as the reservoir pool came up and was lowered. Another such boom was placed downstream from the old town of Rexford near Sullivan Creek. Coyle was intrigued to discover that prevailing winds carried the debris north

The Warland Bridge approaches inundation.

43

where it piled up on the upper log boom rather than the one above Libby Dam. He vividly remembers seeing in 1972 approximately three hundred acres of debris resting against the Sullivan Creek boom, most of it coming out of Canada.

Coyle developed a shared sense of purpose on the job as future flood control would save thousands of dollars, not to mention potential lives. But with that sense of purpose, there was also a certain amount of regret, as Coyle watched the river valley being flooded in 1972. He was one of the last to cross the old Warland Bridge, and as he transported some school children from one side to the other, the waters of the new reservoir lapped at the tires of the carryall he was driving. "It was a magnificent valley with lots of history and it was sad to see some of that go. Old settlers had to leave who had spent their whole life there in the valley and you'd helped replace it!"

The positive impact of flood control was felt a scant two years later when Coyle remembered, "the reservoir [coming] up like a rocket! Basically, every place but the Kootenai River basin got hit in 1974." The dam stored the excess water behind it as the tributaries of the Kootenai downstream overflowed their banks flooding Libby. Jim Morey, who was county commissioner at the time, remembers it well as he was taken on a helicopter ride to see the floodwaters cascading out of the Cabinet Mountains and into the valley. He said Flower, Parmenter, Libby, and Granite Creeks created virtual "rooster tails" as the water dropped from the mountains. Morey believed Libby and other downstream communities would have experienced severe flooding on par with the 1948 flood if it had not been for the presence of Libby Dam holding back the river. A lot had been lost but a lot was also saved as the dam quickly proved its worth.

Coyle stated with firmness, "what made the whole project happen was the people working together. There was a common goal and the focus was building it right and the best they could. I've never seen anything quite like it."

Miles Briggs – The invaluable man

One of the individuals immediately impacted by the beginning of Libby Dam was Miles Briggs. He went to work for the Corps of Engineers in October 1966 as a member of the motor pool. A longtime resident who had grown up in Warland, Montana, Briggs had mixed emotions about the construction of Libby Dam. On the one hand he would help destroy his former home and the homes of friends, but he was also given an opportunity to build a future for himself away from the dominant timber and mining industries of the region. He watched in fascination as the dam rose from bedrock, stretching from canyon wall to canyon wall, slowly taming the river and changing the landscape.

For a member of the motor pool, Briggs spent quite a bit of time on the reservoir in a boat. As the water began to pile up behind Libby Dam, there were some families living on Canyon

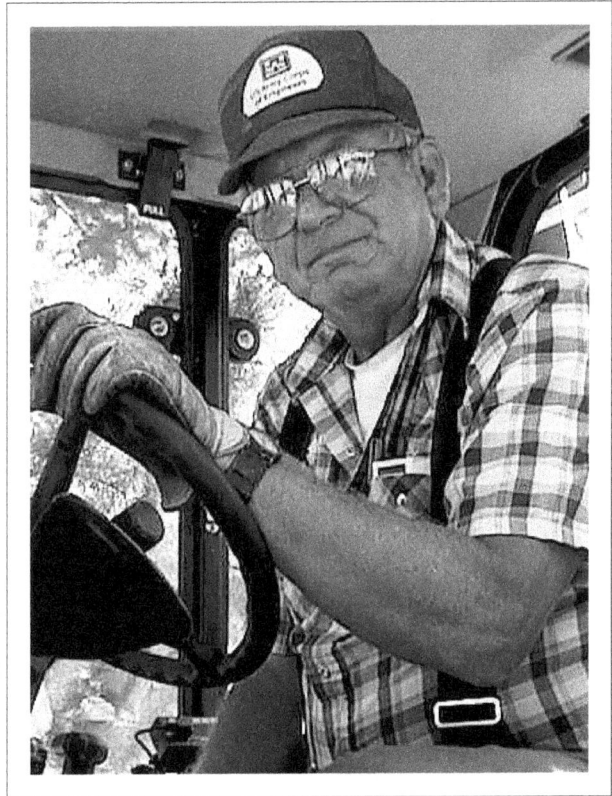

Miles Briggs was the first person to swim in the new reservoir, though not by choice.

Creek who were cut off, for a short period of time, before the new highway could reach them. The Corps provided them with a radio for emergencies, and Briggs would take a boat, accompanied by a sheriff's deputy, to deliver the mail to these residents until more traditional methods could resume. This marked the beginning of numerous water adventures for Miles.

Once the reservoir filled, Resident Engineer Cole looked with irritation at the tops of trees sticking out of the water above the blue line elevation of

Bold Legacy

2,282 feet. It would not due having a forest of mocking treetops sticking out of the new reservoir. He ordered Coyle and Briggs to tidy things up.

They each took a sawyer out in a boat to "log" the reservoir. Jimmy Baker agreed to run the chainsaw, while Briggs operated the boat. They worked from the dam up the reservoir, putting in ten, twelve, and fourteen hour days to complete the task. Briggs and Baker worked off the old Albeni Queen, which had a closed bow on it so Baker had to work from the back. This required Briggs to run the boat up into the branches of the trees sticking above the waterline for his sawyer to cut off the offending tops.

One day Briggs worked the boat into the top of a giant cottonwood tree as Baker cut the branches. Unbeknownst to them, as the weight was dropped from the top the branches came together underneath them until their boat was sitting about two feet out of the water. Briggs recognized what had happened immediately; he and Baker began trying to extricate themselves from the tree's grip. They jumped up and down to jar the boat free but were unsuccessful. Baker leaned way over the edge and tried to saw them free but in the process almost slipped overboard. Finally, Briggs realized that they had two choices; one, wait a couple of days until the reservoir pool raised enough to float them free, or two, call for help. Briggs called for help.

In a quiet, calm voice he radioed Coyle their location and asked for assistance. Coyle responded affirmatively and Briggs and Baker waited for the inevitable. When Coyle pulled up at the helm of a Boston Whaler along with sawyer Howard "Crash" Seward, Briggs and Baker were greeted by hoots and howls of laughter as their two rescuers laughed until their sides ached and tears flowed. When they regained control, they tied onto the stranded boat and pulled it free of the tree's embrace. Thirty years later, John Coyle still delights in telling this story, especially in Briggs' presence.

It is unknown if Briggs was the first man to get a boat stuck in a tree, but he is certain that he was the first one to go for a swim in the reservoir. One of his duties was shuttling inspectors back and forth across the lake in the course of their duties. On one such trip, the prop became fouled by flotsam, present in every new reservoir. While attempting to clean it, the catch that holds the motor out of the water broke. Unfortunately for Briggs, he was leaning on it when it gave way and in his own words he went "ass-over-tea kettle" into the water.

That does not sound so bad, but his legs remained in the boat and he was wearing a personal floatation device, and the combination of the two conspired to do him in when he struck the water face down. The vest immediately popped him to the surface, but with his legs tangled in the boat, he could not roll over to breathe. Thrashing in desperation, the inspector finally flung Briggs' legs out of the boat and he righted himself, gasping for air. Laughing, the inspector was quick to point out that Briggs had just become the first person to swim in the new reservoir.

Blackwell Flats Recreation Area at Libby Dam.
Wiki Commons Photo by Tony Webster, 2016.

For thirty-two years Briggs worked for the Corps of Engineers at Libby Dam. While other job opportunities arose, he remained rooted in the community as firmly as the dam was rooted in the bedrock of the Kootenai River. He had the satisfaction of seeing the construction from start to finish. As Libby Dam Project Manager, Mick Shea, stated, "A man like Miles is invaluable to the project. Project Managers come and go, but people like Miles are the backbone." Without people like him showing up for work every day and doing his job things would not get done.

Landscape work that started fifty years ago has matured, creating a park-like atmosphere and pleasing to the eye because of Briggs; work on the campgrounds and boat ramps on the river are available for public use because of Briggs; neatly trimmed lawns and clean bathroom facilities are indications that Briggs did his job. Recreation playgrounds, and other areas in Souse Gulch are safe and the echoes of children laughing are reflections of Briggs and his crew's dedication to their jobs. He was given an opportunity to learn different skills while working with people of all kinds of personalities, and all the while he made a good living and raised his family. When asked if he would do it again, he smiled and softly replied, "Sure!"

Gene Scalf Morrison-Knudsen concrete foreman

Before construction of the dam could begin, the river valley bottom needed clearing down to the bedrock. Once exposed, the bedrock was scoured clean and the cracks grouted to ensure that no lift from the bottom would threaten the structural integrity of the dam. In Phil Cole's opinion, the surface of the bedrock was clean enough to eat off it and therefore, ready for concrete. Once this task was completed Gene Scalf, concrete foreman for Morrison-Knudsen, the prime contractor on the dam, arrived in Libby with his family and began work in 1967.

During the pouring season, which started in March or April and lasted until the cold weather shut them down in October or November, Gene worked an eight-hour shift, one of three such shifts, placing the four-yard buckets of concrete for the pours. When a bucket was dumped, his four-man crew moved in with ninety-pound vibrators to consolidate and bring the air out of the concrete. The buckets were attached to one of the six cranes, or "whirlys" as they were called, which operated on an elevated trestle that rose

The cab of one of the "whirlies" that placed concrete for Scalf.

were built and the "green cut"[1] made before the next one was started. When the cold weather shut them down in November, Scalf was put to work doing odd jobs such as shoveling snow, cutting keyways, and placing heat tapes in the dam. As construction jobs went, according to Scalf, it was considered safe and the pay was good for the time.

The number of concrete crews working was determined by the weather. One crew would start the season, building up to three at the height of the work season and as fall approached, they scaled back until the project was put to sleep for the winter. With the dam completed in 1972, Gene moved with Morrison-Knudsen to Idaho and continued to work for them for almost thirty years before retiring. When asked about the most fascinating aspect of working on a project like Libby Dam, Gene replied, "all jobs are fascinating. The best job in the world is the one you're leaving and the one you're going to."

Getting the bedrock ready for Gene Scalf.

with the height of the dam. Some of the most difficult pours, according to Scalf, were those located down under the trestle the whirlys ran on. A single pour usually required more than one day to complete and each crew worked on it in succession.

The crews used coolant pipes and ice to aid the curing process of the concrete. The workers did their jobs on the run, grabbing a sandwich for lunch and keeping work going. Galleries and elevator shafts were put in before the pours were made; forms for the new pour

---

[1] This is the process of removing laitance, a chalky weak layer, from the surface of concrete joints to ensure strong bonding between layers of concrete. *Development of the Green Cut Machines and their Application for Dams.*

Don Smith – I've had it up to here with this job!

Donald Smith came to Libby in 1967 as an electrical inspector; the only one on the site for some time. He had seven years of experience working with hydroelectric facilities and wanted to get to Montana, so when the job opportunity at Libby Dam project came along he jumped at it—"I wanted to get back to mountain country" and Libby was "exactly what I hoped for." Temporarily quartered at Reese's Trailer Court, the family wanted to find a place to live once Don retired and Libby seemed a good place to put down roots, so the next spring they purchased a house in Woodway Park.

As an electrical inspector, he oversaw the placement of conduit, relays, and conductors throughout the dam and powerhouse constructions. As the only journeyman electrician, he also got called out on all kinds of projects, including repairing office fixtures, wiring public address systems, working on washers and dryers, and doing electrical work in government trailer houses from Eureka to Libby. Then one day Phil Cole tapped him to han-

dle the job of rigging the Elk Mountain Tunnel holing-through ceremony. His job was to create the necessary connection between the telephone lines from Washington D.C. and the relay in the tunnel that would detonate the charge.

To make sure the ceremony went as planned, Smith had a twin-engine airplane placed at his disposal to fly him anywhere he needed to go to obtain the necessary equipment and materials for the job. Smith loved that airplane and looked for opportunities to get in the air. Unfortunately, working on a tight schedule, he proved too efficient using the materials on hand and the airplane remained grounded.

To ensure the success of the operation he had a bypass switch he could close manually if something went amiss. He spent the night before the operation in the tunnel testing his system, ensuring that when the moment arrived everything would work flawlessly. As he worked through the night, Cole radioed him and asked what he wanted for dinner and Don ordered a sandwich and a quart of buttermilk. During the night he decided to save the buttermilk until the next morning and drank a soda instead.

Just before the ceremony started, he drank about half of the buttermilk and then the ceremony unfolded. President

Johnson pressed the button in Washington D.C., there was a slight delay, and then the charges detonated and the two tunnels became one. As Smith returned to the dam site later that morning, Cole radioed to congratulate him on a job well done. He then asked him how he managed to stay so calm during the ceremony—Smith replied that he had drank a half quart of buttermilk, and in fact was finishing off the other half as they spoke. Cole responded, "The next time we do one of these things get a quart for me too!" Smith said, "I felt pretty proud about the whole thing. It was a workday though, and that afternoon I had to fix a washing machine up in Eureka, so you go up quick and come down quick."

Don Smith did every electrical thing imaginable, from fixing washing machines to installing turbines.

Unlike some of the Corps employees who only stayed for a short time or until the dam was completed, Smith worked on the powerhouse as well. Construction on it began in 1972 when the contract was awarded to Halvorson Mason. Smith worked closely with Burke Electric Company who installed the hydro and communications facilities for the powerhouse. Working as a test inspector, he oversaw the contractor's work on the generators. According to Smith, it took about two years to install a generator, test it, and get it spun up on the system to produce electricity. One time a schoolteacher asked him, "Does it change the taste of the water taking the electrons out?" Keeping a straight face, he patiently explained that electrons were not removed from the water, but that the water was only used as the force to spin the turbines.

While working on the powerhouse in 1973, Smith was assigned to a graveyard watch on the project in March. It seems that in protest for what was happening on the Pine Ridge Reservation at Wounded Knee, South Dakota, the Kootenai from Bonners Ferry, Idaho had threatened to take over the Libby Dam site. Those assigned to the double duty were instructed to not interfere if a takeover occurred, only to observe and report. Nothing came of the threat except some lost sleep.

Installation of the pentstocks that send water to Dan Smith's turbines.

When it came to relaxing and recreating, Smith was busy working on building a house along the Kootenai River. There was Tuesday night bowling and slow-pitch softball to help relieve some of the pressures of the workplace. Cole also got him involved with the Plummer School PTA. Cole then volunteered Smith to do a little research on what it would take to install a new lighting system for the Libby High School football field. Researching the project, he discovered a company that had a four-pole unit with a seven-light array per pole that sat behind the bleachers so that the view of the field was unobstructed.

The system cost $35,000. He gave his research to Cole, who responded, "Okay Don do it. The school has about $8,000 to spend." Smith went to work.

Working in his spare time, he got the St. Regis Paper Company to donate four 35-foot poles that were placed at the football field. One of the contractors placed stakes in the field to align the individual lights for the best effect. Smith had to place all the conduit on the poles and said with a bit of pride in his voice, "All my boys were busy with baseball and whatever. I didn't have any help to put the conduit on the poles—it took a lot of physical labor—so my daughter, Brenda, helped me!"

The new lighting system was looked on with skepticism. Many who doubted the lights would provide adequate illumination of the field showed up at 11:00 pm one evening to watch as Smith flipped the switch. Head football coach of the Libby Loggers, Doc Sargent, arrived as well to see for himself. The moment of truth had come. Smith said, "I threw the switch and that thing lit up like you can't believe! It was just beautiful." According to him, "The contractors and Corps really kicked in on projects like that." The system was still being used in 1999 when the school honored Smith with a plaque for his work.

When asked what the best thing about working on the Libby Dam project, Smith said the people. The interaction was extremely good and everyone worked to a single purpose: to get the job done and done right. He credits Phil Cole and his consummate skill at handling people for the high level of cooperation and camaraderie on the project and for promoting projects that helped the communities of Lincoln County.

Smith recalls having some trouble with an engineer from the railroad when they were working on the signal and communications for the relocation. Smith was putting in twelve hour days, working seven days a week and every time he turned around this guy from the railroad was sending deficiency reports on him to Cole. However, by the time the reports reached Cole's desk, Smith had resolved the issue and it was no longer a problem.

One day Smith showed up for work and was sent to assistant resident engineer Jim Ramsey's office. When he got there Cole was also present. Ramsey held out the latest deficiency report and asked Smith what he knew about it. In frustration he replied, "I've had it up to here with this job," motioning to his neck.

Cole stepped up chest-to-chest with him and responded gruffly, "Do you know what to do in a situation like that?" Realizing he may have pushed too hard, Don refused to back off, he stepped even closer until the two men's noses were almost touching and stated firmly, "No sir I don't know what to do about that but I'm open to suggestions!" Cole glared back and then suddenly turned, ran across the room and jumped up on a chair and said, "Now it only comes to about here," holding his hand waist

Dan Smith's kids are Libby Loggers.

agement acumen finessed an emotionally charged situation, diffused it, and left everyone scratching their heads and wondering what all the fuss had been about in the first place.

For nine years Smith worked on the Libby Dam project before moving on. He kept his roots in Libby though, where all his children had graduated from high school. His house completed, he took jobs outside of the government and traveled all over the country, meeting many of the same people he worked with on the Libby project, but he always returned to Libby. "Every time I leave and get back, I think, boy! I made the right choice building here. I wouldn't trade this spot for anything." Like it did for a lot of Corps employees, Libby became home.

high. Ramsey and Smith both stared at their boss, nonplussed, and the tension immediately drained from the room.

Walking back across the room Cole asked, "Now what're you going to do about this?" Don answered, "Phil, I've already taken care of it just like everything else that guy has written about." Cole said, "That's what I thought," and promptly left the office. Smith cites this as only one example where Cole's man-

---

John Davidson
Libby Dam's institutional memory

Arriving a year after Don Smith, John Davidson worked as an Electrical Engineering Technician for the U.S. Army Corps of Engineers. He brought his family to Libby in 1968 and started working in the Electrical Engineers office, where he checked the drawings of the contractors to make sure that they were meeting the required specifications concerning codes and materials. But like a lot of Corps employees, he did more than one job during his employment at Libby Dam. These jobs included overseeing the re-grouting of some of the anchor bolts on the reservoir bridge and working with the Montana Historical Society researching and collecting artifacts for the Libby Dam Visitors Center.

The latter job was one that he had volunteered for, and it required evening work and the use of his own personal time to complete. He worked closely with groups from Eureka, Rexford, and Warland to preserve the history of the valley once it was inundated by the reservoir. His reading of *Nuggets to Timber,* the early community history of the Libby area, piqued his interest in the history of the area and led to his later involvement in the development and construction of the Heritage Museum in Libby.

Davidson immersed himself in preserving Lincoln County's history, and traveled to Fort Steele, British Columbia with the Montana Historical Society staff to borrow artifacts for display in the new Libby Dam Visitors' Center. Donald Spritzer, who was writing a history of the Kootenai River titled *Waters of Wealth,* mined Davidson's knowledge of local history in his search for photographs from the local museums for inclusion in his book.

Among the things that Davidson took an interest in was the steamboat era on the Kootenai River. When the Corps of Engineers constructed a scale model of a steamboat for the Visitors' Center, Davidson took it around to the grade schools to educate the kids about their heritage. He related an incident when a youngster asked him, "if it would hold a hundred people why did it only have two lifeboats?" He then explained to the inquisitive young mind that the smaller boats were in fact workboats

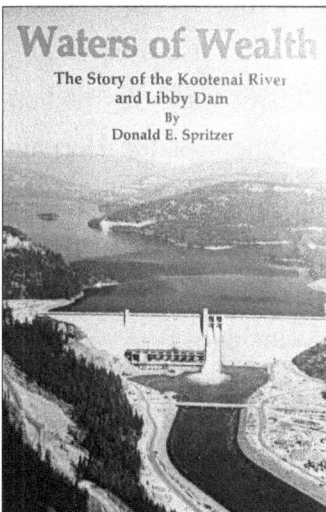

John Davidson was a prime source for Donald Spritzer's Waters of Wealth.

The book was recently republished by Libby Dam Association (at right).

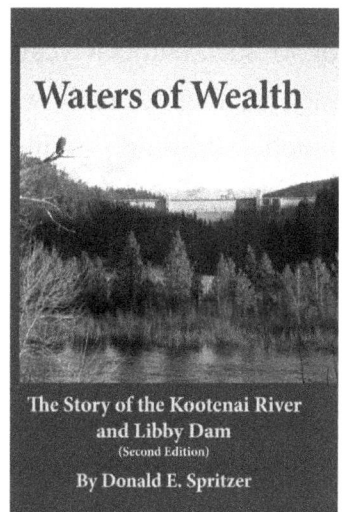

Bold Legacy

John Davidson (center) oversees the final touches on the steamboat replica.

was never much mention of him at the dam and the committee in charge of choosing the names decided to name the bridge after David Thompson because of the symbolism of crossing over the bridge from one side to the other portrayed Thompson's crossing over the border from one country to the other."[1]

and not lifeboats. If a steamboat got into trouble, it tried to run aground on a sandbar or the bank before it sank.

John had the distinction of serving longer than any other Corps of Engineers employee on the construction phase of Libby dam, working from 1968-1983. He stated, "That was simply unheard of to spend fifteen years on a temporary job that normally would have only lasted four years." With his longevity, Davidson knew a few things that many people had forgotten. When asked why the bridge below the dam was named for David Thompson he replied, "there

Canadian David Thompson 1957 commemorative stamp.

As far as he is concerned the impact of Libby Dam was nothing but positive. He remembers residents of Bonners Ferry coming to the dam after its completion and lauding the security it provided for their community downriver. Not only did he have the satisfaction of seeing drawings and plans become a reality in the field, but John also found a home, a place where he and his wife could raise their family. His passion for history and his dedication to the development of the Heritage Museum are still as strong as they were when he first volunteered to help preserve the history of the Kootenai River Valley all those years ago.

---

[1] David Thompson, as an employee of the Northwest Company, was the first Euro-American to explore the length of the Kootenai River, gaining valuable intelligence regarding the headwaters of the Columbia River system.

Bill Glenn – Garbage collector of oddball jobs

The people employed by the USACE worked as perennial problem solvers, who did not hesitate to roll up their sleeves and get their hands dirty. Bill Glenn, a civilian engineer on Libby Dam, exemplified this mentality. He and his wife Evalene had traveled through Libby in 1958 and liked the country; knowing that the construction would start on the proposed dam soon, they decided to transfer to Libby for Bill's next job. He and his wife and son lived in a government trailer house at "Tex" Reese's Trailer Court. Glenn worked on the relocation of Rexford, specifically the construction of buildings, roads, and utilities that the Corps assumed responsibility for at the new town site. Like John Davidson, he also had more than one job. The one he remained most proud of involved his work on the schools in Lincoln County.

The Corps of Engineers had predicted the influx of construction workers would overwhelm the capabilities of the Lincoln County public school system, and it addressed the issue by building additions on existing schools and building new ones. Glenn participated in the construction of additions to Plummer and McGrade schools, and the building of a new mid-

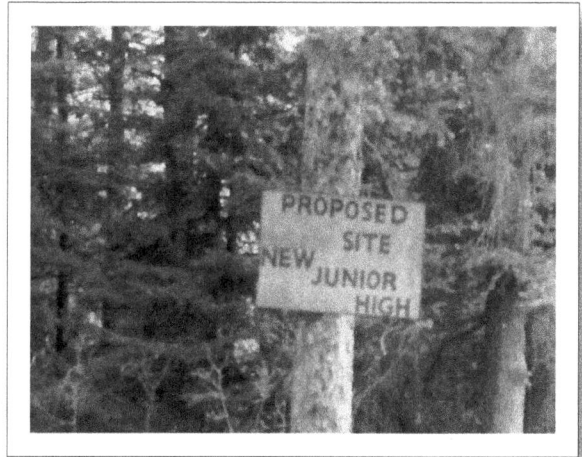

Building new schools was one of Bill Glenn's "oddball" jobs. Ski Dale (under construction below) was the new Junior High.

57

Trego School was expanded as well.

dle school in Libby. Additions were made at schools in Eureka, Rexford, Trego, and Stryker; the Corps provided additional classroom space for any community where construction workers brought their families . For Glenn, this work proved the most satisfying, especially the Libby Middle School, stating firmly, "she's still there, isn't she."

Bill also did follow on work, overseeing small contracts that involved projects such as seeding highway and railroad banks. He considered himself the "garbage collector" for the various oddball jobs that occur on projects of the magnitude of Libby Dam. As Glenn approached retirement, he and his wife Evalene decided to buy a house in Libby, a decision some of his co-workers considered foolish. They warned of the economic folly of buy-

ing during a construction boom, as the bust that inevitably followed would impact the future value of the home. It was the same hard lesson learned by some of those who had worked on Grand Coulee Dam in Washington State.

Bill and Evalene ignored the dire predictions of friends and co-workers and forged ahead with buying their house and making Libby their home. When asked why they chose Libby, Bill stated bluntly, "what was here is why we wanted to stay." Evalene quietly backed him up adding, "we love it here."

The one drawback to working on the Libby Dam project, according to the Glenns, was the flooding of the valley. The fishing above the dam was excellent, and Evalene recalled, "what impressed me about the river was that it had that beautiful color, aqua-blue, from the glaciers." As for the positives, it brought in jobs, not only construction work, but also new shops and stores that contributed to the economic stability of the community at that time. The relationships they formed were also special. Bill Glenn said it was "one of the most get along groups I [ever] worked with."

58

Harold Carbine photo

Scores of the hundreds of men workng on Libby Dam line up at the base of the dam. At least one of them seems to be happy to be at work.

Twelve • A Year in the Life – 1971

There were several hundred men working on Libby Dam at any one time during the construction. Most of these men worked for contractors, and when the job was over they moved on to the next. Also, for most, this was not their first time working on a dam, so there were rarely big surprises in store for them whether they were contract laborers, foremen, or Corps of Engineers employees. An engineering job of this scope neces- sitated a drive for redundancy and perfection; any detail left out could have disastrous impacts in terms of injury, quality of life or taxpayer dol- lars wasted. Construction projects of this size faced a myriad of problems big and small every day, a constant re- minder that no matter how careful the planning, the unexpected could and would occur. Nowhere is this more evident than in the challenges and suc- cesses of early 1971.

59

A Dirty Shame

On January 31, 1971, a quiet Sunday morning at the project, a mass of rock measuring 150 feet wide, 300 feet long, and 80 feet deep let loose above the left abutment and crashed into Libby Dam Builders main power sub-station, destroying it and damaging the refrigeration plant, ice plant, and the re-screening tower, while knocking out the starlight system that provided lights for construction work above the dam. A security guard heard the noise as the rockslide came down and radioed in news of the event. There were some lucky breaks in connection with the slide. First, the construction road and refrigeration plant prevented the slide from smashing into the dam itself; and second, it happened on a Sunday in January when the area was free of workers. As one of the busiest sites on the entire construction project, if the slide had occurred during the peak of the season the event could have proven fatal.

Engineers had previously identified the fault above the abutment during the initial survey but calculated it would hold and had rock bolts inserted as an extra precaution. However, when the construction later began on Highway 37, the "toe" of the fault was cut off. Along with unseasonably warm temperatures and rain, this caused the fault to give way and shear off the rock bolts as it rumbled down the mountain. The February 4, 1971, issue of

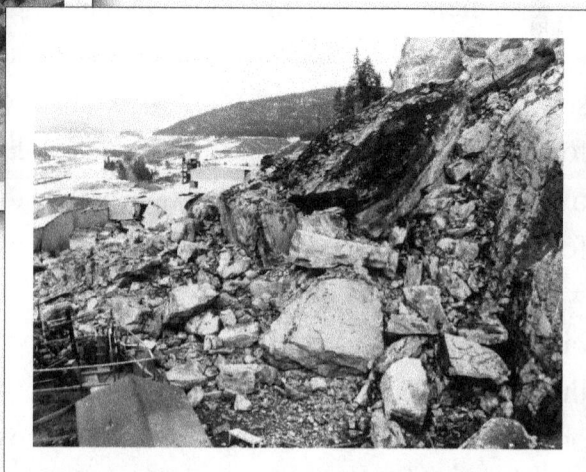

Above: The Dirty Shame slide viewed from the bottom. Some of the boulders are building size. At right: Looking north (upstream) across the slide. Note the line of the reservoir clearing.

The Western News reported that resident engineer Cole was hopeful that "the removal and repair would not delay the April 1 start date designated to begin pouring concrete." With only nineteen percent of the work left to finish the dam, Libby Dam Builders put out a maximum effort, working two crews to clean up the slide area so repairs could begin on the substation and refrigeration plant.

As for the slide area itself, engineers had tendons inserted through the unstable rock to stable strata deeper in the mountain, anchoring it firmly in place. To monitor the continued stability of the slide area, instrumentation was attached to the mountain to record any shifting or destabilization of the area (it is monitored closely to this day). Bad luck and gravity created havoc that day, but fortune smiled on Libby Dam.

Extensometers were installed to monitor ground movement. They are still in use today.

Below: The grid pattern is the pins placed to keep the rock in place. The size of the slide is demonstrated by comparison with the pickup in the lower left corner.

Water and Earthquakes

Equipment to Measure Quakes At Libby's Koocansa Reservoir

By FRANK NORBERG
Missoulian Correspondent

LIBBY — Special instruments

that has been constructed. He
said most of these have been
minor quakes that have occurred deep down inside the

line that will be active 24 hours
each day throughout the year
according to Bob Gadd, local
manager

personnel in interpreting
readings and in preparing
final report on the project
According to Taylor, the

A headline from the February 16, 1971 Missoulian

A wide variety of factors had to be considered in tandem with the building of the dam and the impoundment of water behind it. With the creation of a massive man-made lake, precautions were implemented to monitor the impact it would have on the surrounding area. Seismic events were common with the creation of such large artificial bodies of water, and past projects had revealed that the tremendous weight of the water kept behind a dam would trigger numerous earthquakes as the earth's crust absorbed and adjusted to that weight. For this reason, an instrument array was placed around the reservoir site to monitor seismic activity as the pool filled.

Dr. Gary W. Crosby of the University of Montana's Geology Department and Gene Taylor of the U.S. Geological Survey (USGS) placed an array of instruments stretching from twelve miles downstream of the dam all the way to the Canadian border, because as Dr. Crosby informed *The Western News*, "the disturbances were not always directly under the lake." Via telephone lines and microwave signals, the array provided baseline data readings that mapped the seismic activity of the area prior to the impoundment of the water.

Selective Withdrawal System

Although a late addition to the construction, the installation of the selective withdrawal system proved a unique innovation to the dam. Libby Dam Builders received the Phase One contract for the new system, which required the placement of a "series of concrete structures with removable bulkheads around each of the eight penstock openings." Placed on the upstream side of the dam, the selective withdrawal system allowed the Corps to draw water from various depths of the reservoir for release downstream after passing through the powerhouse generators. This means the Corps of Engineers can regulate the downstream temperature of the river, below the dam. Removing water from different levels of the reservoir keeps downstream temperatures at the optimal level for fish and other aquatic life living in the river.

According to *The Western News* June 10, 1971 edition, the Corps chose the system from several other options because it was the "only practicable solution for Libby Dam at its present advanced stage of construction." They anchored the multi-bulkhead structure to the upstream face of the dam using reinforcing bars grouted twenty feet into the dam. The later addition of post-tensioning facilities provided additional support.

Phase One of the selective withdrawal system was completed down to the low pool elevation of 2390 feet. Phase Two and Phase Three completed it above the full pool elevation of 2459 feet, including bulkheads, trash racks and a gantry crane. The gantry crane can be used to place and remove the bulkheads, as needed, at an average rate of twenty minutes for removal and storage. The gantry crane design allows it to carry out this task with a single worker. The system has now become a standard apparatus on dams and retrofitted to most older dams, according to Cole.

In terms of effectiveness, Fish Wildlife and Parks biologist Greg Hoffman stated, "for its intended purpose it [the selective withdrawal sys-

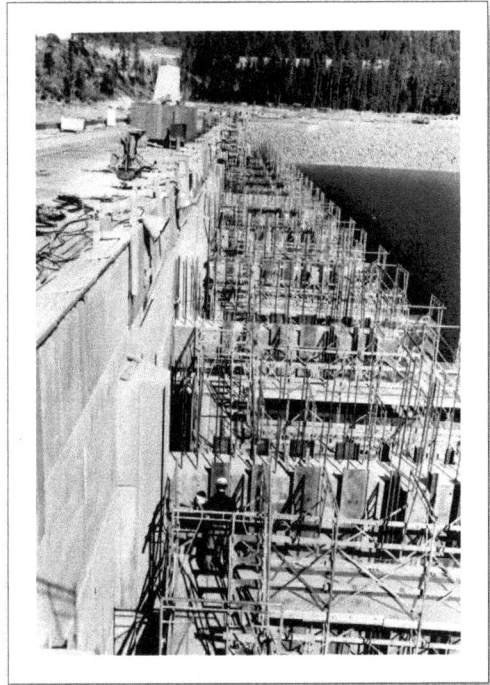

The selective withdrawal system allows water to be drawn through the turbines from multilple levels below the lake surface. Upper right: Framework supporting construction of the higher portals. Below: Portals near the base of the dam.

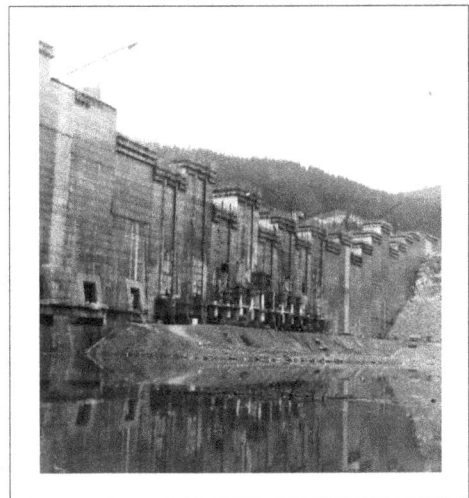

tem] is effective . . . for trout, providing cool water in the summer time and warmer water in the winter." Although costly, it preserved the fishery of the Kootenai River to such an extent that the river remains a Blue Ribbon trout stream. Jack Housel, Jr., gave significant weight to that designation in 1998 when he hauled in the Montana record for rainbow trout (at a whopping 33.8 pounds) while fishing at the base of Libby dam. Fishermen, past and present, line the banks or float the river in drift boats— often in the shadow of the dam—hoping to hook the big one that does not get away.

Reservoir Clearing

The preparation of the reservoir pool, prior to flooding, required a major effort on both sides of the international boundary; initiating timber sales in Montana and British Columbia to harvest the merchantable timber in the river valley started the clearing process. Four times the merchantable timber was harvested below the blue line of the reservoir pool, according to Bill Glenn, and in some cases portable stud mills cutting eight-foot two-by-four dimensional lumber were set up on the clearing site to expedite the process. Any trees that would be left entirely underwater could be left or cut at the discretion of the contractor. Trees above the blue line of 2282 feet were removed, along with all brush and structures. The brush and wood structures were pushed into piles and burned according to safety regulations. Stumps between full pool elevation

Everything above 2282 feet elevation was to be removed. Trees below that level completely under the flood line could be left at the contractors discretion.

2439 and 2459 were removed for aesthetic reasons. Once the clearing contractors had removed all merchantable timber, the heavy work began.

Bulldozers, jammers and sawyers began clearing twenty-eight thousand acres to accommodate the reservoir pool. These men worked efficiently and skillfully, many having done clearing work of this magnitude in the past. One clearing contractor attached a large section of anchor chain between two bulldozers and drove forward, ripping everything in their path out of the ground.

On steep areas, where it was safe, they did "Yo-yo" operations. A D8 bulldozer was positioned on solid ground above the site, then a D6 was attached to the larger machine's winch line and lowered down the steep grade plowing up brush and trees as it went down. Although it sounds more than a little dangerous, Miles Briggs and Bill Glenn both pointed out neither man nor machine was lost during this process.

Anything four inches or over in diameter and eight feet long was removed either by burning or burying,

Above: Brush and small trees were piled systematically to be burned. Below: the "yo-yo" system of clearing required a D-8, a D-6 and two operators who knew what they were doing.

including houses, bridges, chicken coops, outhouses, and barns. Herman West, a reservoir clearing contractor, made brush piles 400-500 feet long and 40-50 feet high for burning. John Coyle remembers West firing up six bulldozers and lining them up, side by side, and pushing the brush and small trees into huge piles, recalling "these guys knew what they were doing." Coyle only remembered one accident during the entire clearing phase.

The clearing, however, was not carried out in a linear progression according to Coyle. The section done by John Collins, another reservoir clearing contractor, around Five Mile and McGuire Creeks was done early and ended up short of the blue line. This resulted in Brigg and Coyle having to complete the remainder of the task, which Coyle described as "two weeks from hell." Even with issues like this, the Americans outpaced their Canadian counterparts clearing the reservoir. Glenn attributed this to their better access to heavy equipment for the job.

The Shutdown

The size and complexity of Libby Dam and its various projects required workers from a variety of the trades such as carpenters, painters, plumbers and pipefitters, operating engineers, ironworkers, electricians, and laborers. At this time a good number of these individuals were represented by a union local affiliated with an international organization. Occasional disputes occurred between workers and their employers, which brought action by their representative union. One such incident happened in April 1971 as construction on the dam was entering its final stages.

Some of the wives of electricians who were members of Local 768 of the International Brotherhood of Electrical Workers employed by Hahn Electric, a Libby Dam Builders subcontractor, set up an informational picket to educate

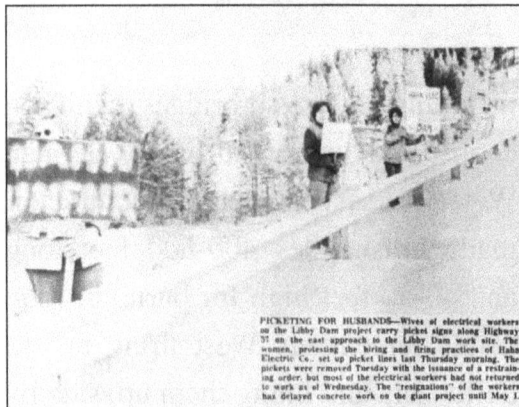

Work Delayed at Dam . . .

Federal Court Intervenes in Electrical Workers Walkout

PICKETING FOR HUSBANDS—Wives of electrical workers on the Libby Dam project carry picket signs along Highway 37 on the east approach to the Libby Dam work site. The women, protesting the hiring and firing practices of Hahn Electric Co., set up picket lines last Thursday morning. The pickets were removed Tuesday with the issuance of a restraining order, but most of the electrical workers had not returned to work as of Wednesday. The "resignations" of the workers has delayed concrete work on the giant project until May 1.

The Western News

Devoted to the Development of Libby and of Lincoln County

Libby, Montana, Thursday, April 22, 1971   Price 15 Cents

other workers about what they perceived as the unfair hiring practices by their husbands' employer. The women accused Hahn Electric of hiring out-of-state electricians over local ones and releasing the Montana electricians without cause.

An IBEW union representative stated in the April 22, 1971, edition of *The Western News* that the international union did not sanction a work stoppage, as a no-strike clause in the contract between the union and Hahn Electric Company prohibited walkouts and work stoppages. The shutdown came at a critical juncture as the project was just beginning to gear up for the big summer season. Assistant resident engineer, James Ramsey, predicted that there would be no "concrete work before the end of the month," since the electricians had been working on several "primary jobs that [were] key to the start of concrete work."

In an act of solidarity, union members from the ironworkers and pipefitters working on the job refused to cross the picket line for two days, before returning to work the following Monday. Legal steps were taken to get the workers back on the job, and Federal District Court Judge Russell E. Smith issued a temporary restraining order against the picketers until a

hearing could determine whether the informational picket by the local union members' wives was legal. In this case, the IBEW and Hahn Electric Company joined as co-plaintiffs against Local 768 and the eight female defendants. In the meantime, the Corps waited anxiously for the settlement of the dispute so work could resume.

A federal court ruling upheld the earlier issued temporary restraining order blocking the right of the women to maintain their informational picket. Judge Russell E. Smith of Missoula, Montana, stated in the ruling that the picketing was in direct violation of the collective bargaining agreement between Local 768 and Hahn Electric Company, and therefore the informational picket could not circumvent the contract's no-strike clause. By April 29, 1971, *The Western News* reported that around twenty of the twenty-two electricians were back on the job and that ". . . the situation at the project [was] quickly returning to normal."

Every day, month, year, and phase of the Libby Dam project had its challenges and successes (the former dealt with head on, the latter celebrated), but always the work continued. Everyone could hear a ticking clock in their head as worked to meet the completion deadline.

Thirteen • Putting Down Roots

Working five and six days a week USACE employees, contract workers, and bosses needed time to step away from the pressures of the job, relax, have a beer, and enjoy some quality time with family and friends. Most of the workers found time to engage in some type of recreation to relieve the tensions and routine of the job.

The Riverside Inn, built by Zook Brothers Construction Company, one of the contractors working on the Forest Development Road, constructed the Inn on the west side of the Kootenai River, near its junction with MT 37, offered a place for men and women to let their hair down. The Inn catered to married and single people alike, with an atmosphere primed for a good time. Entertainment came in the form of go-go dancers, and the Inn served a mean dinner that satisfied its customers. Its proximity to the dam site proved an additional benefit.

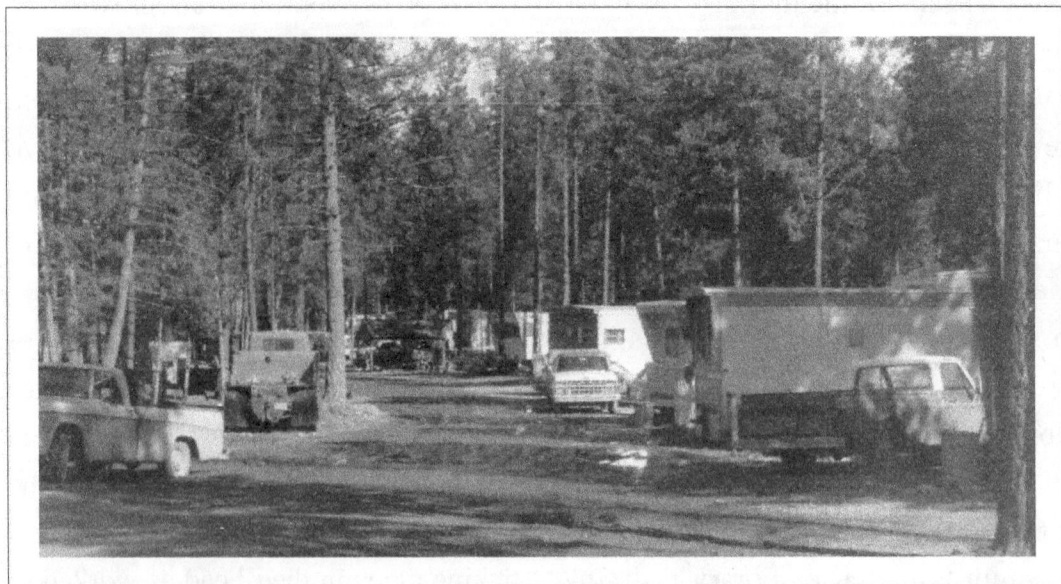

Some trailer parks weren't as orderly as others.

Of course, the Riverside was not the only restaurant/lounge in the area. Other local establishments such as the Big Bend, Gopher Inn, Buck's Frog Pond, Cedar Creek, and the Antlers offered opportunities to mix, mingle, and enjoy some good food. The Antlers, located between Libby and Troy, offered diners the unique opportunity to order fresh trout from their outside pond. You could choose the size of the fish you wanted to have for dinner that night based on the size of your appetite.

When asked what the ladies did to break up their days, Evalene Glenn responded that those living at Reese's Trailer Court had daily canasta games after the kids were sent off to school. Pinochle and bridge clubs offered diversion for the more serious card players, while others bowled in leagues at the Play Lanes bowling alley. They also joined the Libby Women's Club, PTA, and participated in Boy and Girl Scouts. For those wives that had training as nurses and teachers, they were quick to find employment in Libby and surrounding communities. As Evalene recalled, "it seemed like we did something every weekend." Boredom was rarely on the day's agenda.

The outdoors provided the major source of recreation for most. Families

DINE -- DANCE
AT

RIVERSIDE INN

CAFE, LOUNGE, MOTEL, TRAILER COURT

Located 12 Miles
Northeast Of Libby On Highway 37
IN THE HEART OF LIBBY DAM CONSTRUCTION

RESTAURANT HOURS:
Monday - Friday, 6 a.m. to 10 p.m.
Saturday, 6 a.m. to 3 a.m.
Sunday, 12 noon to 8 p.m.

PHONE NUMBERS:
293-6393
293-9412

enjoyed picnicking and fishing excursions where they could slip away from everyone else and just enjoy one another's company outdoors. The Kootenai River above the dam construction delivered excellent fishing opportunities for families such as the Coyle and Glenn to take advantage of before the dam flooded the valley. Some families even visited the clearing sites on the reservoir, marveling at the size of the equipment and onsite stud mill operations

Of course, hunting season came in the fall, and Bill Glenn remembered that just

69

The Sport Is The Thing

A word of consolation to those of us who will return home opening day with little or nothing to show for our efforts: It's not whether you win or lose but how you play the game. Besides, it's a long hunting season. Those poor guys who

fill up early will have to stay home and watch television or put up storm windows, rake leaves, clean the garage and the basement and worst of all will have to listen to us tell about the big ones we hit and the bigger ones we missed.

about every pickup on the project had a gun rack in the back window and at least one rifle hanging from it. It was a common sight in the community that did not alarm locals. Phil Cole enjoyed the hospitality of Ed Boyes' cabin on the Fisher River during hunting season and traveling to eastern Montana with the Fennessys to hunt antelope and mule deer. His family liked skiing, so they spent some time on Turner Mountain, and then traveled to Schweitzer Mountain in Idaho and Big Mountain in Whitefish, MT. As he succinctly put it, "we didn't have any lack of things to do."

Community Involvement

The members of the Corps of Engineers living in Libby during the construction years developed a vested interest in their community, resulting in the establishment of the Heritage Museum. Ernie Moon came up with the concept, and Floyd Lucas designed the building. Miles Briggs used a bulldozer to skid the logs, while Cy Jones and his wife helped peel them. John Davidson also volunteered his personal

time, and the museum became a labor of love for him.

Although their assignments were temporary in most cases, that did not

LOG STRUCTURE PLANNED

A model now, the Libby Heritage Museum will, its sponsors hope, take real scale shape this summer. Initial displays will be housed in converted Forest Service buildings. Fund raising campaigns will be initiated to fund cost of new museum building estimated in neighborhood of $50,000.

stop USACE employees and contractors from donating time and labor to the museum's establishment. Even their grade school kids got into the action, spending part of a day picking rocks from the site as part of a springtime field trip and learning some of the early history of the area.

Helping to develop the Turner Mountain ski area was also a pet project that Corps employees got behind; they worked to clear the ski runs and kept the antiquated T-bar lift in operating order. In Cole's mind, these attachments made it better for everyone. It was easier for local people to accept the newcomers when they saw them rolling up their sleeves and helping on projects that would benefit the entire community, and it helped dispel feelings of distrust and suspicion. Everyone benefited from the interaction.

Boom and Bust

One of the chief concerns for the communities of Lincoln County, as the projects wound down, revolved around the potential severity of the economic impact after all the workers and their families moved on to the next project. The construction of Libby Dam and its co-projects brought a boom to the area reminiscent of the gold rush era of previous decades[1].

The Corps tried to help the communities of the Kootenai Valley mitigate the impacts of the boom as painlessly as possible, as the rapid influx of job seekers, workers, and their families stretched community housing to the limits and swelled classroom sizes to the bursting point. Even with the expansion of schools, construction of housing developments, improved water and sewer infrastructure, road repair, and community enhancement, residents of Stryker, Trego, Fortine, Eureka, Rexford, Libby, and Troy knew the bubble would burst, and they needed to prepare for the inevitable bust.

In 1970, the workforce on the dam swelled to a staggering 2,110 people. The projections for the next three years, according to Seattle District Commander Colonel Howard Sargent, Jr., would drop by half each subsequent year and taper off sharply thereafter as the project was completed. With the completion of the Great Northern

[1] *The Western News*, Libby, MT, 21 August 1975.

Bold Legacy

The Trego school was enlarged to accomodate the "boom, (above) and the Libby Loggers got a new home (at right).

Railway relocation in 1970 and dedication of the Lake Koocanusa Bridge[2] a year later, the decline in the number of workers and their families proved precipitous.

The Corps predicted the average number of workers for 1971, 1972, and 1973 at 1,000 during the summer months with about 500 remaining on the job during the winter. The number of employees on the dam in 1974 averaged 700 and in 1975 that would drop to around 300. These numbers included the workforce necessary for the powerhouse construction which would begin sometime early in 1972.

With 1976 designated as the completion date of the powerhouse, the Corps estimated only an average of 100 employees that year.

According to *The Western News* May 13, 1971, Lincoln County workers "insured by the Employment Security Commission had the highest average income in Montana," from 1967-1970. Averaging $7,982 compared to the state average of $5,948, the county's average had increased steadily from 1967 to 1970 by almost a $1000 per year. Construction workers posted the highest average wage bringing in $11,561 in 1970, with the state average

---

[2] The bridge is Montana's highest and longest, standing 290 feet tall and 2437 feet long. Montana Attorney General Robert Woodahl dedicated the bridge in November 1971, calling it a "perpetual symbol of the cooperative spirit between [Canada and the United States]." *The Daily Inter Lake*, 07 November 1971.

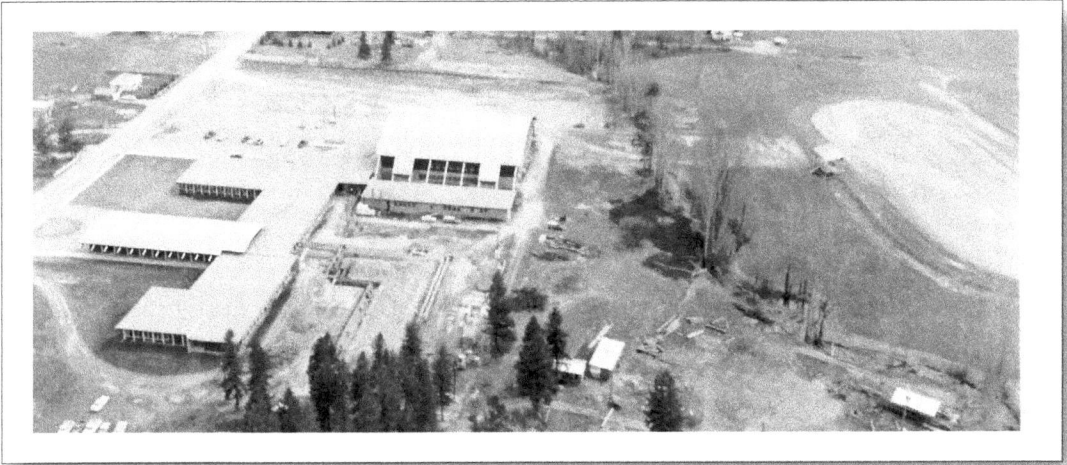

at $8,491. Libby's economic largesse rested on a three-legged stool of construction, mining, and logging. One of those legs was about to fold.

Understanding the economic disaster this could cause the county, from inception the Corps of Engineers had planned a staggered phase out of the various projects. In Cole's estimation, "the phase out was gradual enough that economic impact wasn't terribly dramatic. There was still work going on such as the powerhouse and smaller contracts on Souse Gulch and McGillivray campground." Former county commissioner Jim Morey agreed with Cole's assessment stating, "they came in stages did

the job they were supposed to do and left in stages. I don't think they created that big of an [economic] impact [on the community]."

". . . We made a living before they came — we made a living after they left." In fact, Morey continued, "There was less police then, than there is today. It was increased some but not as much as you would think." The construction boom had come and gone without significant shocks to Lincoln County's economy (major shocks would come later with the closure of W.R. Grace, Asarco, and the sale and downsizing of the St. Regis Paper Company mill and woods departments).

Fourteen • Dedication

Construction on the powerhouse began in 1972, with an estimated completion for 1976. However, Colonel Eineigl, Corps of Engineers Seattle District Commander, knew his time in that position was limited and pushed for the completion and dedication of the powerhouse and dam by 1975. While contractors worked on the powerhouse and dam, John Coyle and Miles Briggs, the latter now working for "Captain Crunch," pushed their maintenance crew into high gear in 1974 and 1975 to complete the grounds work. This included the completion of the Libby Dam Visitors' Center and outdoor recreational areas in Souse Gulch. They groomed trails, set up the stage and podium, and placed chairs and garbage receptacles to accommodate the anticipated crowd for the August 24, 1975, dedication.

John Davidson, co-chairman for visitation, scheduled programs and tours for the public to begin once the dignitaries completed their walk through of the dam. They estimated 5,000 people would attend the dedication, as President Ford's advance Secret Service detail reconnoitered the grounds to determine the security measures they would need to implement for the visit. It seemed all the trucks owned by project employees had gunracks in the rear window with at least one rifle in view, causing President Ford's Secret Service detail consider-

The August 24, 1975, Missoulian got the day and time right, but missed badly on the location of the dam.

extreme northeastern Montana

Staff Photo by Harley Hettick

Libby Dam in extreme northeastern Montana will be dedicated today as President Gerald Ford throws the switch on the first of eight generating units. Dedication festivities begin at 10 a.m.

Ford Arrives in Kalispell at 12:05

Libby Dam Dedication Today

able concern and making them very hesitant to schedule the presidential visit[1].

Security measures were tight, as Coyle remembers. A couple of incidents really stood out for him. The first involved the use of empty fifty-five gallon drums for traffic barricades. Each barrel was duly inspected by

The sun came out just in time on Dedication Day.

a member of the Secret Service, who would shine a flashlight through the two and a half inch bunghole to make sure that the barrel did not contain an explosive device or caustic agent. Then in the agent's presence it was filled with water and the bung was reinserted and tightened with a wrench. Coyle, Briggs, and their co-workers delighted in referring to the individuals who oversaw this part of the operation as "bung hole inspectors."

When asked by one of the Secret Service agents if he planned on attending the dedication, a local member of the night watch flippantly responded, "Oh, I wouldn't get within shotgun distance to them." He was quickly searched and taken to town where he spent several hours being in-

terrogated. His innocent colloquialism almost landed him in jail.

The major threat, however, came from the weather. It had rained for two days before the dedication, and the Corps employees had worked themselves to a frazzle only to watch in dismay as a drizzle threatened to spoil the ceremony. Several of them went to the Riverside Inn for breakfast the day of the event, after having worked all night on the project. The clouds were socked in, and it was still raining. When they came back out, the clouds had broken, and the sun was doing its best to brighten the day. Coyle heard an unidentified crooner come on over the radio singing "Oh it ain't gonna rain no more no more!"

In the wake of the 1970s energy crisis, the dedication of Libby Dam going

[1] Less than a month after his visit to Libby Dam, President Ford survived two assassination attempts while visiting California.

75

online for power production was a harbinger of hope. Among the dignitaries who attended were Governor and Mrs. Tom Judge, Senator and Mrs. Mike Mansfield, Colonel and Mrs. Eineigl. John McIntyre, a noted actor who had starred on the television series *Wagon Train* and a resident of the Yaak Valley, served as the master of ceremonies.

President Ford in his remarks applauded the electrical power output generated by Libby Dam, which would alleviate some of the pressure being exerted on non-renewable resources such as fossil fuels. Canadian Minister of Energy, Mines and Resources, the Honorable Donald S. MacDonald, agreed. Despite detractors on both sides saying "we could have done better . . .", MacDonald did not believe that was true—they had done a fine job. He advocated for continued cooperation between both nations to find viable solutions to the energy problems that plagued their respective countries.

With that, the two men flipped a large wooden switch that signaled the operator, Cliff Silcox, to put Generator One online for power production. Ford and MacDonald remained hopeful that both sides would continue to resolve future crises as they arose over the dam's operation.

At the back of the crowd, stood Troy residents Alex and Vi Cummings with their grandchildren Kim and John. Vi had brought the family camera in hopes of getting a photograph of President Ford, seemed reluctant to push to the front of the crowd and turned to her granddaughter Kim for help. Handing the camera to the twelve-year-old, she urged Kim to move in front of the stage and take the President's photograph for her. The usually precocious young lady however, shrank from the task unwilling to put herself the center of attention, handed the camera back to Grandma Vi and remained firmly rooted in place.

Also sitting in the crowd watching President Ford speak was the mother of a Kalispell doctor who had recently treated John Davidson. He had told Davidson during a medical appointment that his mother had never seen a president, and Davidson arranged for two tickets for the doctor and his mother to sit in the front row.

From concept to paper to reality, Libby Dam took 27 years to complete. Although more work remained to bring the rest of the generators online, the dam had already made a positive impact on the area. In addition to holding back potentially threatening floodwaters in 1974, it now began meeting its full potential with the production of hydroelectric power.

Koocanusa begins to fill the valley, flooding many a whistle stop town.

Fifteen • Under Lake Koocanusa

The creation of Lake Koocanusa proved no small undertaking either in the construction of the dam to start the inundation, or during the required negotiations with the homesteaders, business owners, and community residents who occupied the land destined to become the new lake bed.. The federal government bargained buyout agreements of sufficient sum to mitigate the cost of the years of sacrifice and labor required to put down roots in the valley. Missing from the balance sheet, however, was compensation for the emotional upheaval people dealt with in losing their homes and way of life.

People sell their homes all the time, but it is an entirely different thing to sell a home destined to be bulldozed into a pile, burned, and then drowned. Once they accepted the reality of moving, there was no going back. "Home" would slip below the rising wate —and "childhood" memory would fade rapidly as physical traces of their youth disappeared. In recognition of the importance of remembering our history and the sacrifice made, this section is dedicated to those places that now rest silently under the waters of Lake Koocanusa

Sixteen • Whistle Stops

The area between the confluence of the Fisher River and the Kootenai River north to the Canadian line was a place that saw only sporadic development until the first decade of the twentieth century. Large deposits of coal discovered in the area around Fernie, British Columbia, prompted James J. Hill, owner of the Great Northern Railway, to tap

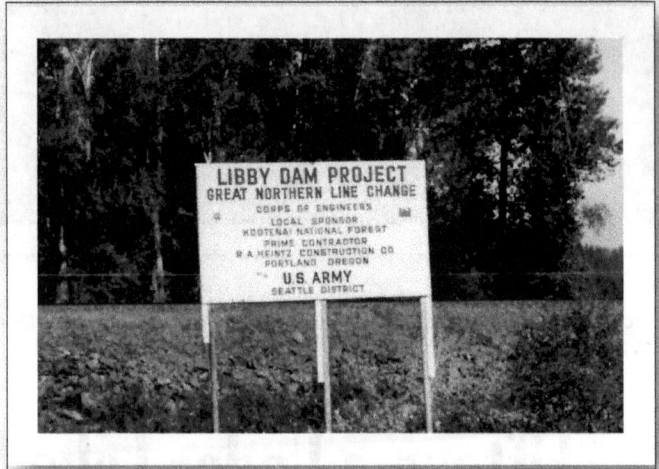

Besides towns flooded by Koocanusa, miles of the mainline Great Northern had to be replaced.

into this market, taking business away from his old partners, now competitors, who owned the Canadian Pacific Railroad. As such, Hill authorized the construction of an extension line from Jennings, MT, upriver to Fernie, B.C. Railroad construction began in 1901 and took a year to complete.

The Kalispell Bee (18 July 1902) announced the opening of the extension line listing the stations between Jennings to the border with Canada: Yarnell 5 miles, Warland $10^{1/2}$ miles, Volcour 16 miles, Ural 20.5 miles, Tweed 25.5 miles, Stonehill 31 miles,

Rondo 38 miles, Rexford 42 miles, Hayden 47 miles, and Gateway 51.7 miles. Maintenance for the extension line required the establishment of stations approximately every ten miles for section crews to use as a base of operation along the route. Each crew was responsible for six miles of track on both sides of the station they were assigned.

A sense of permanency for the small communities growing up around some of the stops was reinforced in 1904, when the Great Northern decided to close the line over Haskell Pass and build a cut-off between Columbia

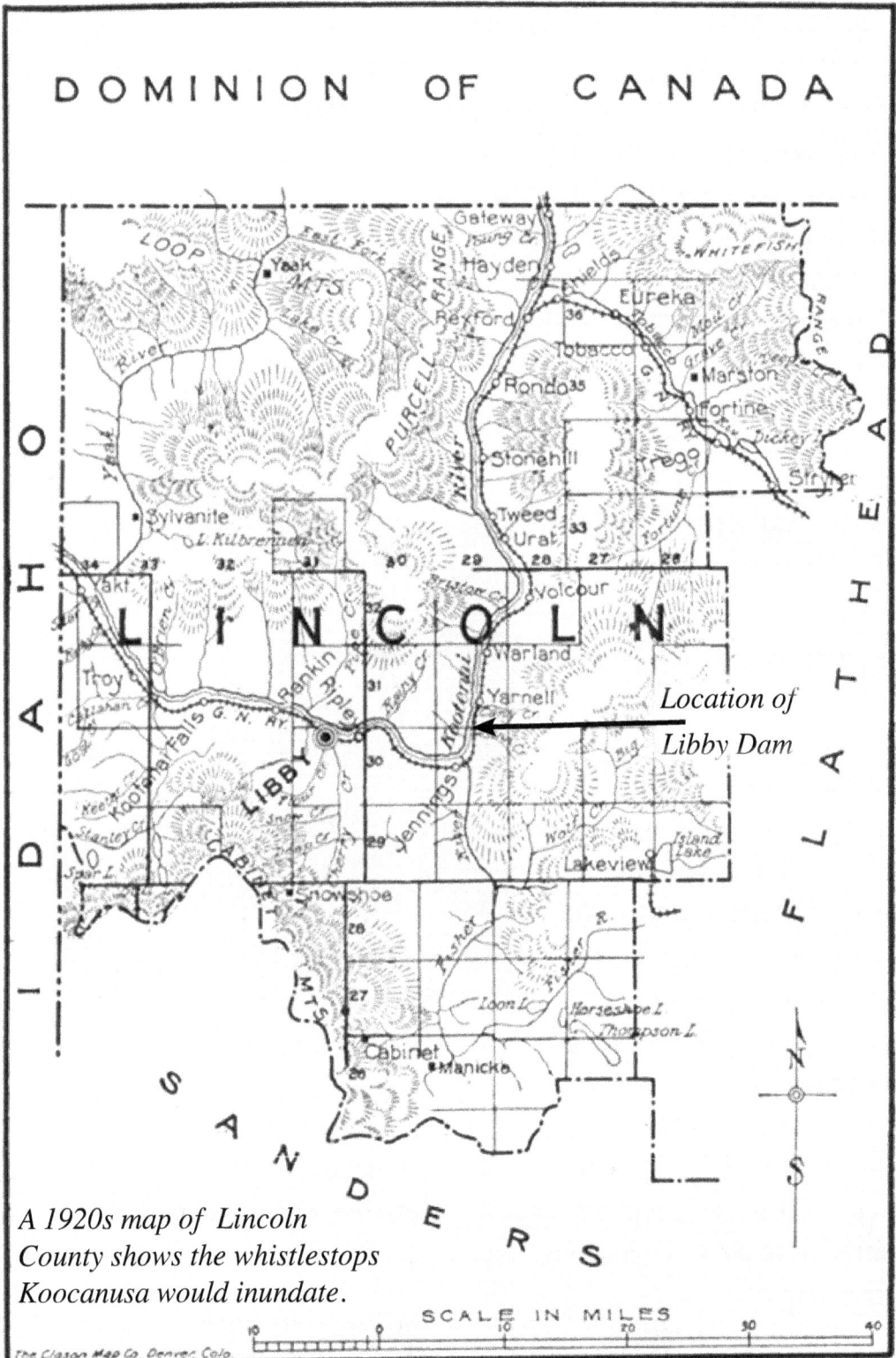

Location of
Libby Dam

A 1920s map of Lincoln
County shows the whistlestops
Koocanusa would inundate.

MAP OF LINCOLN COUNTY, MONTANA

79

Bold Legacy

Falls and the new extension line. The new route provided easier grades than the existing route's short steep grades between Jennings and Kalispell.[1] This new main line down the Kootenai River from Rexford to Jennings and on to Libby provided an opportunity for local boosters to promote settlement and development.

side of the river to Yarnell, as it would require more money to build due to the amount of rock work required to blast the road through to the town. He also pointed out that a road on the north side of the river would serve more people.

Along with the Baird-Harper Lumber Company's promise of $10,000 for the construction of a bridge at Warland, that left Yarnell marooned on the wrong side of the river from the highway, as

---

Yarnell

Some of the railroad stations and sidings along the route could not catch a break when it came to development. Yarnell experienced a brief spark of life in 1920 when discussion arose over the route of the Theodore Roosevelt International Highway along the south side of the Kootenai River, which would have put the small community on a major transcontinental motor route. However, when the district engineer of the Montana Highway Commission reviewed the plan, he would not approve construction of the road along the south

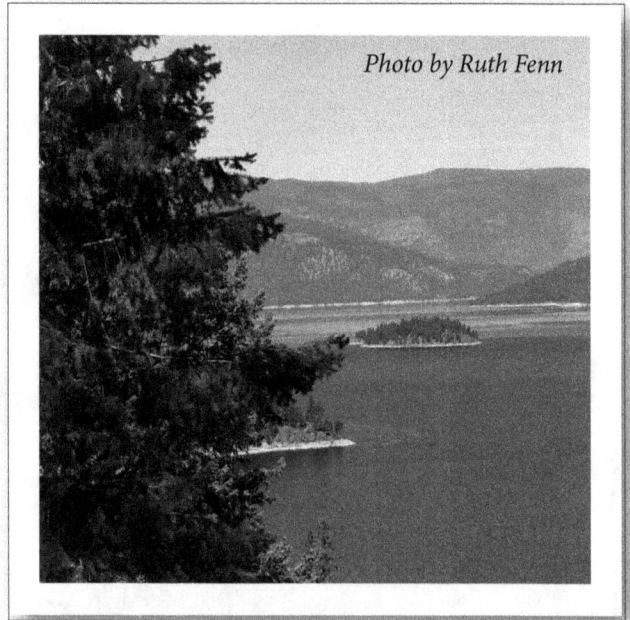

Photo by Ruth Fenn

Yarnell Island is not far upstream from the dam

automobile travel was becoming the preferred mode of transportation in the United States. Yarnell Island, north of

---

[1] Christian Miss, editor, *Historic Overview of The Kootenai National Forest, Northern Region, Libby, Montana, Volume 1* (Northwest Archaeological Associates, Inc. Seattle, Washington, 1994), p. 102.

the dam, is the only remaining marker left today for the old Great Northern Railway station.

Warland

Warland's prospects looked more promising. For years, timber harvested in Canada and Montana was transported downriver via log drives to mills in Idaho or Canada. That changed, however, with the coming of the railroad. Now a mill could ship finished lumber from the area to outside markets, and in 1904 the Warland Lumber Company did so. The new company not only owned the mill, but also the town site and the only store operating in the community. The economy of the upper Kootenai Valley received a much-needed boost with the development of the timber industry, but this would not have occurred without the railroad creating a means to exploit timber resources and ship finished product east and west of the manufacturing center.

With the increase in the town's prosperity, some individuals arrived not looking for work or a business venture to invest in, but to steal from those

US Forest Service achives

Warland in its hayday was a booming timber town.

The Baird-Harper company store at Warland

worker told them no, they returned to the train yard and disappeared. Sheriff Wave Brown, after conducting a weeklong undercover investigation, told *The Western News* that the "yeggmen" had probably escaped on one of the numerous freight trains passing through the area.

The Baird-Harper Lumber Company purchased the Warland Lumber Company mill, stump lands, timberlands, store, and the town site in April 1916. The new owners rebuilt the company store and added a pool hall, hotel, and housing for the married mill workers. This made Warland the only company-owned town in Northwest Montana. The purchase also brought the promise of a hundred new jobs at the mill, plus employment opportunities for cutting timber and building logging railroad lines.

who had. Residents of Lincoln County discovered in mid-January 1916 that the Lincoln County Sheriff's office had launched a manhunt in the area shortly after the first of the year. *The Western News* reportedtwo Yeggmen had robbed postmaster Tom Moore of five hundred dollars."[2] The bold pair accosted Moore when he exited the Warland depot to investigate a strange noise. At gunpoint, they took the money from Moore's hip pocket and promptly hopped the eastbound passenger train, No. 28, to Rexford where they approached a worker and asked if there were any deputies in the area. When the

By purchasing timber sales on Cripple Horse and accessing the area by logging railroad, the company stayed active with the capacity to produce

---

[2] "Yegg" is a slang term that came into use the first decade of the 20th century and popularized by the Pinkerton National Detective Agency. McClure's Magazine, in its February 1901, issue suggested that Chicago detectives should define the term. The article also claimed that hoboes who break into country post offices were classified as Yegg-men. From Etymonline, harvested 23 May 2025

30,000 board feet of lumber a day. In 1917, the mill burned down and temporary equipment was brought in to maintain production while a new one was constructed and completed in 1918. By the end of World War I, Warland had approximately 300 residents and fifty houses. The boom was short-lived. An industry-wide recession in the 1920s claimed the Baird-Harper Lumber Company, and the mill closed permanently in 1926. Portable tie mills dotted the valley as residents sought to make a living, and the town struggled to survive as a service center for independent loggers and settlers.

Warland was considerably shrunk by the time Kookanusa began to rise.

Within two days of his 1933 inauguration, President Franklin Delano Roosevelt called a special meeting of his advisors and created the Civilian Conservation Corps (CCC) to alleviate some of the economic duress gripping the country, and to put at least a portion of the 13.6 million unemployed back to work.

The CCC served a dual purpose: first, to provide jobs for single men between the ages of eighteen and twenty-five who came from families on relief; and second, to begin a campaign against soil erosion and declining timber resources that threatened the existence of natural resource industries such as farming, ranching, and logging.

The CCC assigned eight hundred of these young men to work on various projects throughout the Kootenai National Forest. Some of them were stationed at Libby, Pipe Creek, Yaak, Rexford, Troy, and Warland. Their high level of organization ensured efficiency and productivity. The men assigned to Warland established a camp and began riprapping the riverbank and constructing a bridge across the river. The CCC remained active around Warland until 1942

Their camp did not remain abandoned for long due to a labor shortage on the Kootenai National Forest as a result of the United States declaration of war against Germany, Italy, and Japan. To augment a skeleton crew of Forest Service employees, thirty-seven Italian nationals interned at Fort Missoula were sent to the old CCC camp at Warland in June 1943. As non-combatant foreign nationals from a country at war with the U.S., these individuals found themselves detained for the duration at internment camps for being in United States territory when hostilities were declared.

The men assigned to the camp at Warland had all volunteered for the work and received a wage for their work, which consisted primarily of piling brush. Carl Gilbertson, in charge of this contingent, called the men a "fine bunch of fellows." Detained off the coast of Central America, Captain Gabriel Locatilli told *The Western News* that he had been ordered home by way of Japan and ended up in Fort Missoula. He expressed a high regard for Americans and a strong desire to see a quick end to the war. Despite the economic boom precipitated by the war, Warland once again resumed its outpost role for the US Forest Service, area residents, and J. Neils Lumber Company logging operations on the upper Kootenai.

It was a great place to grow up though, according to Miles Briggs, whose family moved there in 1951. Briggs used to set lines in the river at night and then check them in the morning before school to see if he caught any ling cod. Each spring he watched in fascination as the water tore through the canyon carrying large trees in its swirling waters on its mad dash downstream. While Warland was usually spared from flooding during spring runoff, he recalled, "you could count on Bonners Ferry getting wet every year, just depended on how bad."

When fishing the reservoir near Warland Creek, sometimes he would look down into the water and think, "I used to live down there."

Volcour

Located midway between Warland and Ural, Volcour struggled to establish its own identity. County newspapers reported sporadically on events

WESTERN NEWS.

VOL. VIII   LIBBY, LINCOLN COUNTY, MONTANA, THURSDAY, MARCH 31, 1910   NO. 39

FIRST STEPS TAKEN IN BIG KOOTENAI VALLEY FRUIT LAND DEAL

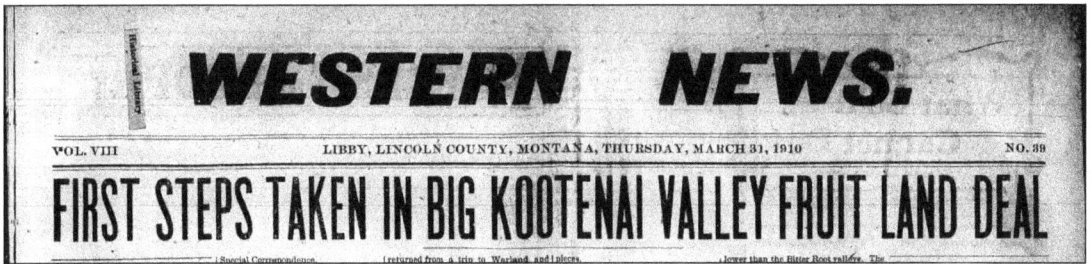

KOOTENAI'S TIMBERED SLOPES TRANSFORMED TO BOWER OF ORCHARDIST

Thrice Favored Section of Northwestern Montana Produces Rich and Luscious Fruit, Ripened in the Mountain Sun— Ample Rainfall and Ideal Climatic Conditions Make Valley of Kootenai a Second Bitter Root—Mountains Clad With Raiment of Snow Tower Above the Growing Valley of Fruit.

occurring at Volcour but under headings that demonstrated its subordinate status to its neighbors. Without even a post office, train traffic sped past the station unless flagged to pick up the occasional passenger.

That began to change after the establishment of the main line along the upper Kootenai. The Great Northern Railway, always looking to promote development along its routes, began releasing reports from Professor Thomas Shaw, who worked as one of the railroads many agricultural experts. Shaw claimed he had never seen finer fruit lands than those available along the Kootenai River. The fertile cutover lands of farmers, ranchers, and lumber companies just needed enterprising individuals to invest in the opportunity.

Newspaper ads in *The Western News* and *Eureka Journal* began appearing in 1910 advertising the sale of land designated as fruit lands. Kootenai National Forest Supervisor Dorr Skeels received applications from several individuals requesting tracts of land for entry as fruit lands under the Forest Homestead Act of 1906. Local boosters from Libby and Eureka promoted this as well, claiming Kootenai Valley fruit, vegetables, and other crops outperformed Washington, Idaho, Oregon, Colorado, Wyoming, and North and South Dakota at the Billings Dry Farming Congress sponsored by James J. Hill.

While local newspapers gushed about the opportunities and the number of individuals interested in developing the fruit industry around Volcour, short growing seasons and marginal soils doomed any such enterprise. Although remnants of the attempt can continue to be seen along the Kootenai between Libby and the dam, Volcour's tenuous existence remained tied to the railroad.

A 1921 picnic near the Ural Great Northern Depot.

Ural

Ural owed its existence to the Great Northern Railway, which provided jobs either working directly for the railroad, or indirectly by cutting railroad ties to sell to the Great Northern. Supplying these ties augmented the incomes of local homesteaders.

Due to the propensity of J.J. Hill to use different ethnic groups on his labor crews, the cultural mix of Ural proved diverse, consisting of Russians, Romanians, Bulgarians, Turks, Greeks, Armenians, Mexicans, and Japanese. In fact, it is speculated that the town got its name from some Russian railroad workers who claimed that the area reminded them of the Ural Mountains of their homeland.

One of the earliest settlers in the area was the Fritch[3] family. Wenzel and Josephine Fritch emigrated to Ural from Czechoslovakia, a satellite state of the Austria-Hungary Empire, in 1904. Claiming land under the Agricultural Settlement Act of 1906 (also called the

---

[3] Immigration records show the family name as Fryc and alternative spellings of Fritsch and Fritch began appearing in newspapers in the 1920s. Jerry applied to the district court in 1940 to legally change the last name to Fritch.

Forest Homestead Act) they acquired a homestead and built a life. Josephine became postmistress of Ural in 1908, and held the position until her retirement in 1940, while Wenzel opened a general store in 1913 that he operated for over fifty years. Their son, Jerry, delivered groceries and mail to homesteads along the river in a canoe. When Fritch opened his store in 1913 the population of Ural was fifty people, the bulk of them employed by the Great Northern.

Jerry and his younger brother Rudi both registered for the draft after the United States entered World War One. Rudi died of an undisclosed illness aboard ship on his way to England in 1918. Jerry spent his time in the U.S. Army stateside and received his discharge in 1919. With the passing of his father Wenzel in 1925, Jerry assisted his mother in the operation of the store and management of land claims. He became postmaster at Ural in 1940, replacing his mother, a

Two Fryc brothers from Ural joined the Army during World War One. Only one made it home.

RS 223 Montana Adjutant General's Office records,
Montana Historical Society, Helena, MT.

position he held until retiring in 1957. With dam construction well on its way, Jerry and his wife, Agnes, left the Ural homestead for good in 1969 and moved to Kalispell.

Like many rural communities of the West, Ural felt the effects of the Great

Bold Legacy

Depression to such a degree that it adopted the nickname "Poverty Flats," as it struggled to survive the decade of the 1930s.

August and Rose Mory arrived in Ural shortly before the birth of their son Jim in 1932. August worked for the railroad until his death in 1934. Rose continued living in Ural, drawing a Mother's Pension, and raising the children until her sudden death at the age of thirty-five in 1941. Although their grandparents and other relatives lived nearby, family friend Primo Paolini, a Great Northern section foreman, took the Morey[4] children in to raise.

Paolini had come from Italy with Jim's father, and they worked on the railroad together until the latter's death. Morey recalled that perhaps one hundred people lived in a two-mile radius of Ural and that the river was about nine hundred feet wide at that point. The town, located on the east bank, had a ferry connecting it to the west shore. The forty-five foot long ferry rested on pontoons with aprons on both ends for loading and unloading wagons and cars. Designed to use the river's current to pull it from one side to the other, it operated by tightening the wheel on one of two cables, turning the ferry to catch the current, propelling it across to the other side.

The river was clear and pristine, as Jim describes it, and a "beautiful blue green." In the spring the river rose and the ice broke up creating a grinding, rumbling noise as the Kootenai fought to free itself from winter's grip. Wading out into the ice-filled waters, Morey and his playmates would swim and ride the icebergs downriver for entertainment.

With only twenty students in the little town's school, the five Morey kids comprised a quarter of the student body. Paolini, who Morey referred to fondly as "Pop," ruled with an iron fist and insisted that the children's chores be done before anything else. Jim had about five hundred rabbits that he had to "pull grass" for every day before school and vividly remembers the day when "Pop" admonished him, "Jimmy either pull grass for those rabbits or turn them loose." Morey chuckled, "I thought that was a pretty good idea so I turned them loose. I still think there're descendants of my rabbits at Ural today!"

Fishing was his favorite pastime. Morey remembers one particular time

---

[4] Sometime after the death of August, Rose began spelling the family name Mory, as it appears on her marriage license, as Morey.

fishing with his brother from McGuire Creek to Ural where, despite throwing back any under a foot in length, they still managed to catch thirty-five fish in one trip. Clarence Kimber used to fish a big hole above town with a cane pole and fill his creel with rainbow trout ranging from eighteen to twenty inches. When young Jim asked what his secret was "he [patted] me on the head and [said] 'patience—just patience my boy.'"

He also recalls during the spring putting a measuring stick in the river and watching the water come up over a foot an hour. There was a large "boil" upriver that they watched in fascination as large logs were sucked into its vortex and disappeared. They learned to respect the river—enjoy it sure, but always respect it. That very same power kept the water clean in Morey's opinion. By tumbling the rocks together, the riverbed was kept clear and the water drinkable.

With no local law enforcement, "Pop" served as the local peacekeeper and broke up more than one fight between fractious railroad workers. According to Morey, the "gandys[5]" would get liquored up on homemade applejack wine, then fists, shovels, and knives would start to fly. Paolini would call the sheriff in Libby and wade into the melee to break it up. By the time a deputy arrived the fight was usually over, and "Pop" was in the process of patching up the walking wounded. No one was ever killed, but "a few ears were cut-off." When World War II broke out and the Italian detainees were sent to Warland, Paolini would go down once a week to talk to the men and see if they needed anything.

It was also a time of instability, as Morey recalls. Men were riding the railroad cars in droves, and more than a few stopped at their house before his mother passed away. They would ask for a cup of water or to do some chore for a sandwich; "Mom told them yes but if they had a stick in their hands they had to leave it behind because the dog would take 'em. It didn't matter, most would keep the stick and when they came through the gate, the dog would be on them and they would be hollering and heading back over the fence." The Morey children and Primo Paolini stayed in Ural until 1948, when "Pop" bid on a job at Priest River, Idaho and moved the family there. Jim returned to Lincoln County in 1960.

---

[5] Gandy comes from the term "gandy dancer." A gandy dancer was a railroad laborer who worked on a section gang and used tools made by the Gandy Manufacturing Company, Chicago, Illinois

Tweed

While most of the stations along this section of the Kootenai had history associated with the area prior to Libby Dam and the reservoir, Tweed is forever tied in a secondary position to Ural, Ural-Tweed and the last native band of bighorn sheep in northwest Montana inhabiting the east side of Lake Koocanusa. Early reports on the bighorn sheep failed to point out the genetic characteristics that set it apart from other bands of bighorn in Montana.

Smaller in size than other native bighorn species and chocolate-brown in color, the sheep lost approximately 4350 acres of range with construction of Libby Dam and creation of Lake Koocanusa. The population, never large, settled at around two hundred animals. After the construction of Libby Dam the population plummeted to twenty-five, creating the real possibility the herd would go extinct.

Attempts to boost their numbers oc-curred several times prior to and after the dam was built, most notably including an effort to populate Wild Horse Island in Flathead Lake. These efforts largely failed as bighorn sheep rely on historic migratory routes between spring, summer and winter ranges and relocating them to an unfamiliar range challenged their ability to survive.[6]

Stonehill

The area around Stonehill proved a dangerous stretch of the valley from the construction of the extension line in 1901. Stories of accidental drownings, train derailments, and shootings (accidental or otherwise) peppered the pages of *The Eureka Journal* and *Western News*. Rockslides and washouts proved the biggest threat to Great Northern trains moving through the area and kept section crews busy with repairs.

Perhaps one of the most bizarre incidents occurred near Stonehill in

---

[6] Gerald W. Brown, *Ural-Tweed Bighorn Sheep Investigation, October 1, 1976 – May 31, 1979*. Montana Department of Fish and Game Report in Cooperation with U.S. Army Corps of Engineers Contract No. DACW67-76-C-0083 Project Completion Report. Harvest from the Internet Archive, 24 May 2025. "Ural-Tweed bighorn sheep make comeback near Libby," *The Billings Gazette*, 21 September 1986; "Sheep habitat restoration," *The Independent Record*, 28 September 1987; "Report On Bighorn Sheep Study", *The Western News*, 01 January 1942.

September 1924 when *The Western News* reported the shooting of Chester H. Collins in the presence of his future bride. Collins parked his car along the river on the Charles Reid ranch and borrowing the boat belonging to the ranch owner, rowed to the opposite shore where his fiancé Miss Irene Peck had her residence. This was a common practice for motorists on the Reid ranch and elicited little or no reaction from Reid in the past.

When the couple returned to the car to head for Libby and their pending nuptials, the car refused to start. The couple knocked on Reid's door and asked for some hot water to warm the engine. Reid refused and ordered them off his property. Retreating to the river bank, Collins built a fire to heat water as Irene looked on. Reid approached the couple with a revolver in hand and ordered them to put the fire out. At that point, the situation went sideways as, according to Collins, Reid fired two shots striking him in the back.

With Irene's assistance, the two retreated downriver to a neighbor's house and reported the shooting to Sheriff Frank Baney, asking for his assistance.

Volume XXIV   Libb

BRIDEGROOM SHOT AT STONEHILL IN PRESENCE OF HIS BRIDE-TO-BE

Irate Rancher Wounds Man Who was On His Way To Be Married.

WOUND NOT SERIOUS

Starting out to be married but meeting with an irate rancher who proceeded to shoot him was the experience of Chester H. Collins, who gives his address as Seattle, Wash. The shooting occurred last Monday morning about 2 o'clock and was done by Chas. Reid, the irate rancher on his ranch at Stonehill. Collins was taken to a hospital at Spokane and, it is said, will recover. Conflicting stories are told by the two principals. It appears that

Mrs. Long Here.

Mrs. Ethel Long of Eureka, republican candidate for the office of clerk of court, spent a few days in Libby the latter part of the week. Mrs. Long is a gracious lady, has a wide circle of friends in the northern part of the county where she and Dr. Long have been well and favorably known for a number of years and undoubtedly will poll a good vote in the general election.

County Will Install Ferry at Ural

Arrangements have been completed

Dr. Morrison accompanied the sheriff up river, stabilized the patient and arranged to have Collins transported to Spokane the next day. Baney brought Reid to Libby to stand trial.[7]

Chester recovered from the wound and on October 4, 1924, he and Irene finally made it to Libby for the marriage license and were married the same day.[8] Charles Reid was convicted of second degree assault and sentenced to the state penitentiary for not less than one year or more than two years.[9]

Stonehill remains a destination for those daring enough to hone their rock

---

[7]"Bridegroom Shot At Stonehill In Presence Of His Bride-To-Be", 25 September 1924, *The Western News*.

[8] 16 October 1924, *The Eureka Journal*, p. 7.

[9] "Charles Reid of Stonehill…", 02 December 1924, *Livingston Enterprise*, p. 7.

climbing skills on the cliffs above Highway 37. Motorists brake and gawk with fascination at the agility of the climbers before rolling past on their way to Libby, Eureka, or across the Koocanusa Bridge to the West Kootenai.

Rondo

The upper reaches of the Kootenai River Valley proved fertile ground for the criminal element, as the remoteness of the area offered ample opportunities for escape and evasion once a crime was committed. Just such an event occurred at Rondo, the scene of one of Montana's most daring train robberies and manhunts.

The Great Northern Railway's Oriental Limited had pulled out of Rexford on September 12, 1907 bound for points west. As the train approached the siding at Rondo, two masked men leaped from the tender into the cab of the engine and ordered Engineer Silas Shutt to stop his train in a rock cut on the other side of the station. Forcing Shutt and his fireman, Fred Pearson, to carry dynamite and fuses, they approached the mail car and knocked.

When threatened, Philip D. Lang and his assistant Robert P. Sims, opened the door and a masked man pushed past them as he ordered them from the car. The remaining bandit stayed outside, firing down the length of the train to keep the passengers inside and out of the way. Setting explosives charges around the express safe door, they ignited the fuses. When the debris cleared, the sides and roof of the car had disintegrated, rendering the train inoperable, and the safe door removed from its moorings.

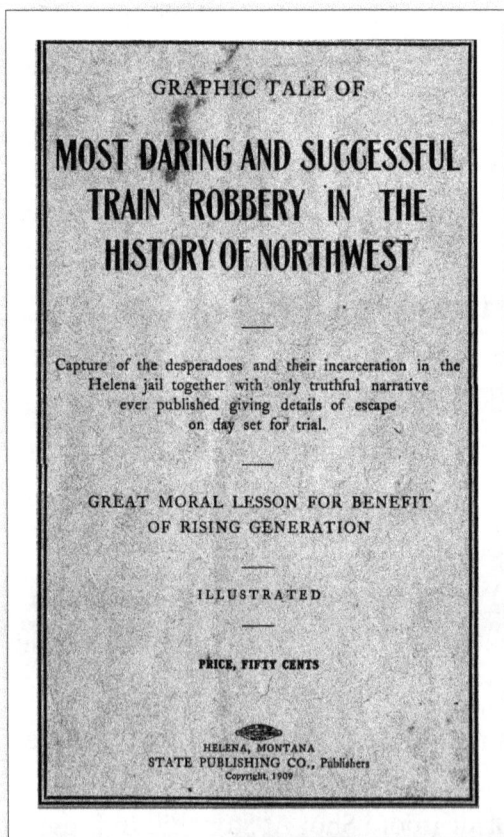

GRAPHIC TALE OF

MOST DARING AND SUCCESSFUL TRAIN ROBBERY IN THE HISTORY OF NORTHWEST

Capture of the desperadoes and their incarceration in the Helena jail together with only truthful narrative ever published giving details of escape on day set for trial.

GREAT MORAL LESSON FOR BENEFIT OF RISING GENERATION

ILLUSTRATED

PRICE, FIFTY CENTS

HELENA, MONTANA
STATE PUBLISHING CO., Publishers
Copyright, 1909

Rondo's claim to fame was published in booklet form.

Disappointed in the contents of the safe, the two men began cutting open U.S. mail sacks and hit paydirt as several of them held bundles of cash destined for banks along the train's route. Taking the money, the two men disappeared into the night. With the mail car destroyed, Pearson walked back to Rondo to report the robbery.

WRECKED EXPRESS CAR.

The remains of the freight car and the unhinged the safe.

Law enforcement tracked them to the banks of the Kootenai, where they then lost the trail. Did the men cross the river to lose themselves in the Yaak Wilds, head east through the Pinkham Creek Breaks, or run north across the Canadian line?

Weighed down by forty thousand dollars of stolen cash, the men did not end up running far and were picked up three weeks later near Bonners Ferry. Extradited to the Flathead County jail, Sherrif Billy O'Connell recovered $14,395 from the men, some of it still in wrappers from the Commercial National Bank of Chicago. After consulting with local law enforcement, federal marshals transported the two men, George Frankhauser and Charles McDonald, to Helena to stand trial in federal court for tampering with the United States mail.

They did not remain in Helena long and soon escaped from the Lewis and Clark County jail. Initial attempts to apprehend Frankhauser and McDonald again failed. Of greater curiosity for locals was how, during the early morning hours of March 21, 1908 , the two men managed to saw through the steel bars of the jail without alerting any of their twenty-five fellow inmates, two jailers, and the deputy sheriff on duty that night. Ten months later, George Frankhauser returned to Helena in cuffs.

GEORGE FRANKHAUSER   CHARLES MCDONALD

Frankhauser died in Leavenworth. McDonald escaped and was never caught.

The trial of Frankhauser lasted several days as evidence mounted against the defendant. His previous incarceration in Montana State Penitentiary further damned him and on January 26, 1909 the jury reached a verdict of guilty on all charges. George Frankhauser was sentenced to a life of hard labor in the federal penitentiary at Leavenworth, Kansas without a chance for parole until January 1924. He died on February 9, 1921, of peritonitis, and with no one to claim the body, officials buried his remains at the Leavenworth Prison cemetery.

Charles McDonald disappeared after the Helena jailbreak and although rumors circulated regarding sightings of the man, he remained at large. Also remaining at large was the remaining $26,605 taken in the robbery that law enforcement never recovered.[10]

---

[10] The unabridged version of this appears "A Hard Man: The Life and Crimes of George Frankhauser," *The Trail*, Vol. XX, No. 1, Spring 2011 #11 (Trego, MT). Gary Jennings, Editor/ Publisher. *Graphic Tale of Most Daring and Successful Train Robbery in the History of the Northwest*, State Publishing Co., Publisher (Helena, MT, n.d.). Author unknown.

Rexford

The town of Rexford is a story of persistence. When the Great Northern pushed upriver from Jennings in 1901, the town shifted location for the first time so it could take advantage of being on the extension line to Fernie, BC. Two years later when the new main line was proposed between the extension line and Columbia Falls, the

Above: Third time's a charm. The new Rexford townsite being prepared.
At left below is a relocated local tavern. At right is the new post office.

Mitigation for Libby Dam included new campgrounds, including Rexford Bench.

town pulled up stakes and relocated a second time one mile to the junction of the two lines. The new town site had a roundhouse and operated as a distribution point for Canadian coal moving east and west. Rexford's future looked bright in 1903.

The Great Northern developed a gravel pit near the town to furnish material for maintenance repairs on the Fernie-Jennings line and provide building materials for the new railroad bed from Columbia Falls. Between the gravel pit and construction crews, it was estimated that the town could see the addition of two hundred new jobs to bolster its economy. At the same time the town itself expanded as new buildings were erected to handle the influx of workers. "The hum of the saw and hammer is constantly heard and there is plenty of work at good wages for carpenters and other builders," *The Western News* gushed in its May 07, 1903, edition.

While Rexford's initial prospects seemed good, reality soon toned down the rhetoric of expansion and the people who stayed settled into making a living far removed from the beaten path. The roundhouse was removed in the 1930s when the Fernie line was taken up.

The town faced its biggest threat when construction began on Libby Dam in 1966. Refusing to see their community die, Rexford residents relocated for the third and final time above the proposed full pool level of Lake Koocanusa. A new post office, school, town hall, fire station, and other required infrastructure was built at the new site by the Corps of Engineers. To honor those communities that succumbed to the rising water of the reservoir new city streets were named Rondo, Ural, Gateway, Hayden, and Warland.

Hayden

The construction of the railroad extension line, 1901-1902, gave high hopes to the promoters of Hayden, a station on the line between Rexford and Gateway that was named for Charles S. Hayden of the Great Northern Railway Company's land department. W.M. Frost, B.F. Berry, Ward C. Lyman, and Nels Bergerson filed articles of incorporation for the townsite company in March 1903. Surveyors were already onsite plating the newest community in the Tobacco Plains. The promoters sought a newspaper for the town to "boom the place."

In the month following announcement of the incorporation of the Hayden Townsite Company, a doctor employed by the railroad looked over sites to establish a hospital for construction and railroad workers. *The Kalispell Bee* also reported "first blood spilled

at Hayden, Geo. Gird put it all over George Breeding", which one can only assume was the result of a street brawl. This prompted Sheriff O.P. Gregg of Flathead County to visit Hayden, looking for an appropriate building site for a jail.

Theft and armed robbery were boon companions in the Hayden area, as *The Kalispell Bee* reported no less than four robberies in one week. Harry Proctor and John Doe Dutch were sentenced to ninety days in the county jail for stealing a half barrel of whisky from

THE FLATHEAD HERALD-JOURNAL

HO! FOR HAYDEN!

THE ONLY TOWN
in the northern part of Flathead county
THAT IS GROWING

Now is the Time
to obtain a choice location for business purposes before the best lots are all sold

Town is Rapidly Building Up
and has a fine country tributary, it drawing upon whole of Tobacco Plains country

The Copeland and Mintier Mining Property just bonded to Chicago capitalists for $30,000, is near Hayden and will draw its supplies from us

We are in the Right Location
and you cannot afford to miss this opportunity of ia fine business site.

HAYDEN HAS TWO SAWMILLS which furnish lumber for all buildings at reasonable prices.

Hayden Townsite Comp'ny
B. F. BERRY, Pres.   A. J. KING, Treas.   W. M. FROST, Sec'y-M'g'r.

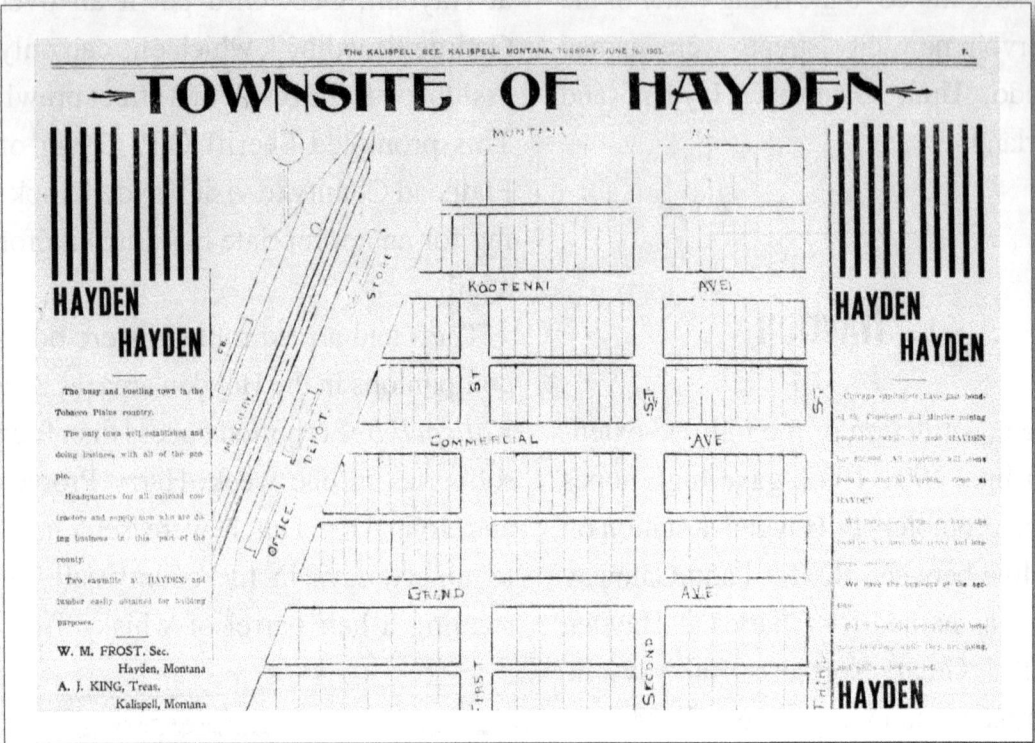

The big plans for Hayden didn't come to fruition.

a box car. According to the newspaper, "the men, with several others got on a big drunk and were having the time of their lives when arrested.[1]" Hayden "bug-juice" served as a willing accomplice for many of the mishaps, robberies, stabbings, and shootings.

Despite the best promotional efforts of W.M. Frost, Hayden's promising future failed to materialize. The post office opened in 1903 and closed two years later as construction workers moved on, leaving empty town lots and abandoned saloons.

Gateway

Gateway was the last train stop north before entering Canada and the first one south when coming into the United States. Its financial success relied heavily on the commerce generated from Great Northern construction crews that filtered in and out of the area working on the Jennings-Fernie extension line. Pat Burns, an area homesteader, sold beef on contract to the railroad to feed the crews, while butchers in Gateway

---

[1] "A Ver Big Drunk." *The Kalispell Bee*, 28 July 1903, p. 5.

"Mulligan pot." While the stew simmered, a dance commenced with the participants dressed in old clothes with a spoon and tin cup hung over their shoulders that clanked in disjointed rhythm to the dancers' steps. When the Mulligan stew was pronounced ready everyone sat down, removed their eating wares from their person, and commenced the feast.

prepared the cuts of meat for consumption by the laborers.

The town gained fame for its "Mulligan Balls" held by the Order of the Sons of Rest.[2] Everyone was invited and all who attended brought vegetables or meat to add to the

When the construction workers moved further north on the line, Gateway's heyday passed. A few businesses remained in operation, serving the rural population that remained. The federal government moved the Customs office to Roosville in 1933 and the Great Northern removed the tracks on the Fernie extension line in 1936. By the time construction finished on the dam and the waters began to rise, not much remained of the community but memories.

---

[2] The Order of the Sons of Rest is a euphemism for those wishing to emulate the hoboes, vagrants, bindlestiffs, Knights of the Road, or anyone who took unsolicited free passage on the freight trains crisscrossing the country.

99

Sixteen • Fish and Wildlife

The small communities that sprang up around sidings and railroad stations were not the only ones affected by the building of Libby Dam. Stump ranches, homesteads, and people who simply wanted to lose themselves in the remoteness of the area were forced to concede defeat in the face of progress, as was the wildlife that made the valley its home.

Whitetail deer, Ural-Tweed bighorn sheep, moose, and mule deer along with waterfowl and other birds were forced to adapt to the changes of landscape and habitat. Spring, summer, and winter range surrendered to rising waters, forcing everything to move higher. The lake did not act alone in this, as the relocation of Highway 37 and the railroad line brought heavy equipment that carved roads out of mountainsides and railbeds through cuts and bored through the mountain. The new route for the railroad down Wolf Creek and the Fisher River impacted wintering grounds for deer and elk, while the new Highway

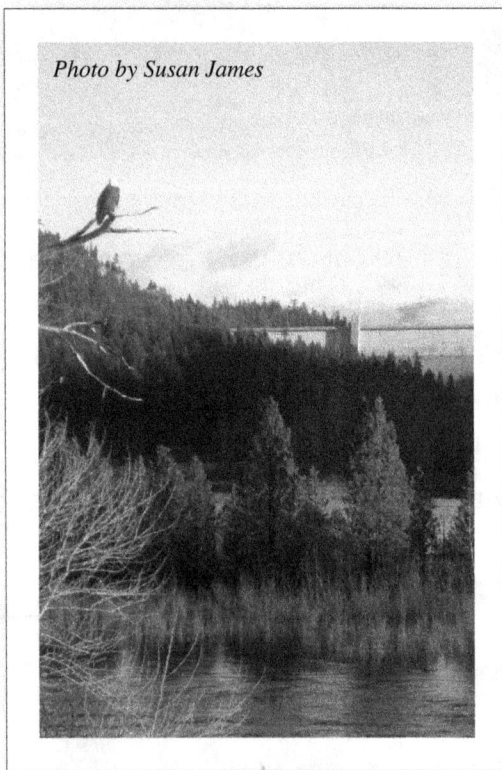

Photo by Susan James

37 disrupted the natural migration of the Ural-Tweed bighorn sheep.

Fish habitat changed as the dam interrupted the cyclical flows of the Kootenai downriver, requiring simulated spring freshets to aid spawning sturgeon below Kootenai Falls. Above the dam, native westslope cutthroat trout, the object of Miles Briggs' childhood obsession,

Construction of the raceways for the Murray Springs hatchery.

became the interloper as Kokanee salmon dominated the reservoir. To balance this disturbance, the Corps of Engineers constructed a fish hatchery at Murray Springs to offset the impact the dam had on native fish populations in the river and its tributaries.

Change brought adaptation, and the passage of years bred acceptance of the concrete structure. Mountain lions now roam in the vicinity of the dam, slipping down to quietly drink from the river's edge as fishermen laugh and joke less than twenty yards away. Eagles and ospreys feed, play, and breed in the shadow of the dam, taking advantage of the river and the lake, and all that they have to offer in the way of food and shelter. Whitetail and mule deer claim the grounds around the Libby Dam Visitors' Center along

with thousands of recreationists who come every year, their raucous noise echoing across the face of the dam.

Blue herons, mirroring the silhouette of pterodactyls, move shyly away from anything that disturbs their tranquility. Turkeys, in all their awkward glory, perch precariously on the railing of David Thompson Bridge and watch with studied indifference the discharge of water through the powerhouse generators. Bears come down from the high country late in the summer to feed on apples from old trees planted by some bygone inhabitant. Raccoons cavort with fisherman on the rip-rapped banks of the river below the dam, threatening to steal fish from the unwary. These sounds and images are the new history being written on the foundation of the old, interconnected but separate.

Seventeen • Reflections 2000

On the twenty-fifth anniversary of President Gerald Ford's dedication of Libby Dam a much smaller crowd gathered to commemorate the event. The landscaping that John Coyle and Miles Briggs rushed to finish has matured, creating a park-like atmosphere. The waters of the Kootenai River no longer tear through the downstream communities of Libby, Troy, Bonners Ferry, and Creston, BC. Recreation and generation of electrical power now overshadow the need for flood control, and in a time of brownouts and rolling blackouts the steady hum of the powerhouse takes on a whole new significance.

Those who have invested and sacrificed the most for progress are the ones who identified the problem and rolled up their sleeves to solve it, accepting the changes that it brought. Old time Ural resident Marvin Green understood this:

I hated it when they put the dam in because I lost all my good fishing. I had more than a dozen super-duper fishing spots along the Kootenai that I could go to any time I wanted, with expectations that I would come home with a mess of trout out of any one of them. But, on the other hand, there's a place down below Libby here, that I have stood in my tracks and never moved on the shore and caught twenty-five. I'd of liked to see the Kootenai stay the way it was before Libby Dam, but you have to have progress.[1]

Inez Herrig agreed.

My Dad [Sam Ratekin] would feel great about the scientific progress. He was a well-read man. I think he'd feel good about the dam providing electricity. The cost was immense, but it was the initial cost.

[1] OH 153 Marvin and Enid Green Interview, May 10 and July 27, 1980. Interviewed by Victor Bjornberg. General Oral History Collection, Montana Historical Society, Library & Archives Program, Helena, MT.

The waters of Koocanusa rise at Warland.

Now it will go on for the life of the dam and produce electricity.[2]

Pauline Harmon (Libby) said:

I think with the coming of the dam, the character of the county changed. It is inevitable because there are so many more people. But it wasn't all bad, because there were a lot of fresh ideas and in many cases, fine things. So many fine people moved in and joined us in the loving of our home.[3]

And by Jim Morey's telling:

People didn't trust the Corps and it was hard for them to overcome. Everybody but me wanted that dam but you gotta give the devil his due—they put it in good! I hated to see the valley flooded. The trade-off for electricity was worth a lot but that old valley was worth a lot too. Ilene and I would drive up to Warland every evening when they were filling the reservoir and watch the water rise up over the top of four

[2] OH 152 Bob and Inez Herrig Interview, April 24, 1980. Interviewed by Jennifer Thompson and Victor Bjornberg. General Oral History Collection, Montana Historical Society, Library & Archives Program, Helena, MT.

[3] OH 166 Pauline Harmon, January 12, 1978. Interviewed by Sherry McKean. General Oral History Collection, Montana Historical Society, Library & Archives Program, Helena, MT.

big spruce trees that grew up around the old house she used to live in.[4]

Phil Cole stated it succinctly. "Most of the real benefits of the project accrue to the folks downstream. The negative impacts of the project accrue to the people on the site."

When Phil Cole came back for the twenty-fifth anniversary celebration, he said that the most memorable aspect for him was the wonderful staff people he worked with during his years on the project. "Dam construction of this magnitude was being phased out in the United States, so we were able to attract some of the best dam engineers that I think were

available." He continued, "after twenty-five years I was real appreciative of the way it looked." But then he smiled and said, "Maybe it's a bit too quiet though."

Voices past and present will continue to swirl around Libby Dam as the floodwaters of another era swirled around the communities of the Kootenai; detractors and supporters will argue until they are blue in the face about the detriments and benefits created by the construction of the dam; meanwhile, the massive concrete structure nestled in the canyon that once caused so much damage to the Kootenai River steamboats continues to do its job, an inanimate object surrounded by life.

---

[4] Interviewed by the author, 2000.

Postscript 2025

Twenty-five years ago, my wife and I stood under the hot sun and listened to dam project manager Mick Shea, Phil Cole, John Coyle and Governor Marc Racicot laud the continued benefits of Libby Dam in flood control and power production. They also spoke about the work they did building the dam, their fond memories of the project, and the stories that still resonated with them a quarter century after the dam's completion. When I met with Mick the following week to discuss the manuscript, he stressed his desire to see a book that rested heavily on the stories. Given the scope of the project, which from start to finished spanned a decade, focusing on stories meant that some things were not going to make the final manuscript.

As such there are some glaring omissions from this book that deserve historical investigation. Chief among them are the Kootenai people's loss of ancestral homelands and cultural sites, and initial negotiations and on-going interactions with the tribe over the management of the reservoir, protection of those cultural sites exposed during the construction, and continual risk from increased recreation.

A close second revolves around community growing pains as residents of the Kootenai Valley adjusted to the presence of the dam and Lake Koocanusa. This should have reached a resolution years ago but given the push and pull associated with management of the Kootenai River ecosystem, those issues will never completely disappear. Evidence of this perpetual struggle occurred a mere twelve years after the dedication of Libby Dam when the Corps of Engineers admitted that it had the worst record of any major dam/reservoir in the Pacific Northwest of reaching full pool, something it had only managed to do five times during that period.

While Libby Dam had its detractors, far more residents of the county supported the project than opposed it. That was not the case when discussions and preparations began for the construction of a re-regulating dam below the confluence of the Kootenai and Fisher Rivers. As the 1980s saw decline and uncertainty ripple through Lincoln County, most of the residents opposed the re-reg dam and its impact on the river and the Kootenai's designation as a blue ribbon fishery.

This is a long winded way of saying there are plenty of stories left to tell, and this book should not be the last word on the history of Libby Dam, but rather additional aggregate for what comes next. In 2050, Libby Dam will turn seventy-five, which is plenty of time for other historians to add to the historical narrative.

Sources Consulted

Libby Pioneer Society, Libby Women's Club, *Nuggets to Timber: Pioneer Days at Libby, Montana,* (Libby, Mont.: Libby Pioneer Society and the Libby Women's Club, 1970).

Christian J. Miss, ed. *Historic Overview of the Kootenai National Forest,* (Seattle: Northwest Archaeological Associates, 1994).

Jack Nisbet, *Sources of the River: Tracking David Thompson Across Western North America*, (Seattle: Sasquatch Books, 1994).

----, *The Mapmaker's Eye: David Thompson on the Columbia Plateau,* (Pullman: Washington State University Press, 2005).

Eugene H. Skinner, "The Flathead Tunnel: A Geologic, Operations, and Ground Support Study, Burlington Northern Railroad, Salish Mountains, Montana," (Spokane Mining Research Center, Spokane, Wash.), Bureau of Mines Information Circular, 1974.

Donald E. Spritzer, *Waters of Wealth: The Story of the Kootenai River and Libby Dam*, (Boulder, Colo: Pruett Publishing, 1979).

Bruce Sterling, Montana Fish, Wildlife & Parks Region 1: Bighorn Sheep Annual Report, July 2915-June 2018.

Philip Van Huizen, "Building a Green Dam: Environmental Modernism and the Canadian-American Libby Dam Project, *Pacific Historical Review*, Vol. 79, No. 3 (August 2020), ppl 418-453.

Compiled by the *Western News* of Libby; with cooperation of the *Eureka Journal* and *Libby Times*, Lincoln County, Montana: History, Resources, Industrial Development and Record in the Great War, (Libby, Mont: Western News Publishing Company, 1920).

Newspapers

The Western News, Libby, MT

The Eureka Journal, Eureka, MT

The Daily Inter-Lake, Kalispell, MT

The Billings Gazette, Billings, MT

Great Falls Tribune, Great Falls, MT

The Independent Record, Helena, MT

The Missoulian, Missoula, MT

The Spokane Chronicle, Spokane, WA

The Calgary Herald, Calgary, Alberta

Lunch break, January 1974.

www.ingramcontent.com/pod-product-compliance
Lightning Source LLC
Chambersburg PA
CBHW062111090426
42741CB00016B/3394